40:HOUSES

OSCAR RIERA OJEDA

THUNDER BAY
P·R·E·S·S

San Diego, California

Thunder Bay Press
An imprint of the Advantage Publishers Group
THUNDER BAY   5880 Oberlin Drive, San Diego, CA 92121-4794
P · R · E · S · S   www.thunderbaybooks.com

All notations of errors or omissions should be addressed to Thunder Bay Press, Editorial Department, at the above
address. All other correspondence (author inquiries, permissions) concerning the content of this book should be
addressed to Rockport Publishers, Inc., 33 Commercial Street, Gloucester, MA 01930-5089. Telephone: (978) 283-9590;
Fax: (978) 283-2742; www.rockpub.com

ISBN: 1-59223-095-4

Library of Congress Cataloging-in-Publication data available upon request.

1 2 3 4 5 07 06 05 04 03

Cover Images:

Front cover:

Top row: Camila del Fierro/Christian DeGroote Arquitectos, Ltda. (left); Guy Wenborne/ Christian DeGroote
Arquitectos, Ltda. (second left & right); Luis Poirot/Christian DeGroote Arquitectos, Ltda. (second right)

Second row: Guy Wenborne/Christian DeGroote Arquitectos, Ltda.

Third row: Luis Ferreira Alves/Eduardo Souto Moura-Arquitectos, Lda. (left); George Lambros/Wheeler
Kearns Architects (second left); Paul Ferrino/Peter Forbes, FAIA, Architects (second right); Scott Frances,
ESTO/ Peter Forbes, FAIA, Architects (right)

Fourth row: Scott Frances, ESTO/Peter Forbes, FAIA, Architects (left); ©Richard Bryant, Arcaid/Gwathmey
Siegel & Associates Architects, LLC (second left); Nick Wheeler/Peter Forbes, FAIA, Architects
(second right); Paul Warchol/Peter Forbes, FAIA, Architects (right)

Fifth row: Nick Wheeler/Peter Forbes, FAIA, Architects (right); Art Grice/The Miller/Hull Partnership
(second left); Gustavo Sosa Pinilla/Lacroze Miguens Prati (second right & right)

Back cover:

Nick Wheeler/Peter Forbes, FAIA, Architects (top left)

Art Grice/The Miller/Hull Partnership (bottom right)

Printed in China
Design: Lucas H. Guerra and Oscar Riera Ojeda
Layout: Oscar Riera Ojeda

Text on pages 8–17 by Michael J. Crosbie

40:HOUSES

OSCAR RIERA·OJEDA

Introduction

by James McCown

"They dreamt not of a perishable home. Who thus could build?" asked William Wordsworth. The idea of the house as a lasting cultural and artistic statement dates back to the villas of the Roman emperors. Many of the great houses of the twentieth century are still known by their original names long after the first owner's demise—Ludwig Mies van der Rohe's Farnsworth House, Frank Lloyd Wright's Robie House, and Le Corbusier's Villa Savoie spring to mind. The house is the most personal of architectural undertakings, and those with the money to commission the great masters wanted more than just a great place to entertain and sleep. They hoped that through an architect's genius they could achieve some measure of immortality.

Here in the early years of the twenty-first century, the notion of the "house" is at once profound and muddled. The unrivalled wealth of the 1980s and 1990s spawned a pervasive obsession with residential real estate. In this sphere, there was no compunction whatsoever in tearing down a house that appeared not to conform to the fashion of the moment or to the perverse and ever-changing laws of "highest-and-best-use" economics. For many, the single-family home became merely another commodity, perhaps a temporary resting place for an upwardly mobile family as it moved from Atlanta to Denver to Phoenix in an endless corporate itinerary of more, bigger, and better. (Along the way the word "house" was largely abandoned, replaced with a hype-filled lexicon trumpeting "contemporary town homes" and "full-service-gated communities.")

And yet the houses presented in this volume, it seems to me, represent the opposite pole—they are designed for clients who want the very permanence and sense of edificial longevity that our society increasingly conspires against. The geographic scope of the collection is vast, ranging from the cool rain forests of Washington state to the wealthy precincts around New York City and Chicago to the windswept plains of Patagonia to the Atlantic coast of Portugal.

In particular, it shines a light on what I believe to be a neglected subject—the rich interpretations of architectural modernism that exist in southern South America,

What can account for the innovative design voices emanating from Chile and Argentina? I grew up on the American Gulf Coast, a region that still retains remnants of its past as a French and then Spanish colony. I remember years ago walking through the French Quarter in New Orleans with a friend from Rome. As we passed the numerous walled residences, which offer only a teasing peak of the opulent gardens and courtyards contained therein, my friend exclaimed: "Spanish! Very Spanish." It is a uniquely Latin idea to turn a rather taciturn face to the world at large and leave the real architectural drama for the inner areas of the house, and this *parti* can be seen in the work of the Argentine and Chilean practitioners chronicled herein. And while the houses' forms at once evoke the great Latin masters like Luis Barragán, they also reflect the influence of early Europeans like Loos and Le Corbusier, not surprising given the Europhilic proclivities of these two Southern Cone countries.

The *norteamericano* architects featured seem equally capable of fresh invention within the modernist vocabulary. There are projects that range from a brave architect's daunting task of "adding on" to a house by Mies van der Rohe to buildings slipped into hillsides in as unobtrusive a manner as possible. The Miesian world of minimalist steel supports and vast expanses of glass—"the world's most expensive wallpaper," as Philip Johnson once quipped—contrast with other houses that seem to take their cue from Frank Lloyd Wright and subsume occupants in a world wholly of the architect's own making. One of the few constants among all the designs is a reverence for the centrality of the hearth—"the happiness of the domestic fireside is the first boon of heaven," as the great statesman and architect Thomas Jefferson said.

This book identifies three distinct regions in the United States that are the nodes of residential architectural activity—suburban and exurban Chicago and New York City and the Pacific Northwest. Modernism has always had an enthusiastic audience in the urban Midwest—could it be the freshwater breezes wafting in from the Great Lakes? In and around greater New York, an early post-World War II infatuation with modernism seemed in the 1980s to retreat into a historicist stupor that slavishly copied a romanticized vision of the Gilded Age. But the 1990s brought a renewed appreciation of the reductionist aesthetic, and firms like Gwathmey Siegel continue to evince modernism's deft ability to reinvent itself. The Pacific Northwest seems beholden to no style or era, and the singular designs it produces seem ample proof of that statement.

But we circle back to the idea of contradictions. Houses designed by well-known architects in stunning natural settings are almost by definition for the wealthy. It used to be that a house would announce its owner's financial position and social station—witness the early twentieth-century Vanderbilt and Astor mansions along Fifth Avenue, and the more recent and much-lamented McMansions dotting new subdivisions around the United States. But in this book, the houses do almost the opposite—they "blend in with nature" to an almost excruciating degree. And yet within these rarified compounds—some complete with helicopter pads, guest cottages, and pool houses—an organic ethos or a an attempt to "blend in" seems a bit disingenuous. Many of the houses seem to be trying very hard to not be what they are: Large abodes for people of means and consequence. The Wrightian notion of a house being part of a hill—neither the hill nor the house the lesser for the bargain—might be appropriate for the truly modest aspirations of some latter-day Henry David Thoreau. But here is it merely a pretentious way of appearing to be unpretentious?

Not all houses will achieve the permanence suggested by Wordsworth. But the home remains, to quote Bernard Rudofsky, ". . . the depository of our wishes and our dreams, memories, and illusions. . . " One wonders whether the poet Philip Larkin was thinking about an exquisitely rendered modernist house when he wrote:

Rather than words comes the thought of high windows:
The sun-comprehending glass,
And beyond it, the deep blue air, that shows
Nothing, and is nowhere, and is endless.

Moore House

Sharon, Connecticut
Alfredo de Vido Architects

The design for this house—on which the owners collaborated with the architect—included the goal of merging it with its natural environment. The site was selected for its beauty, and the house was designed to disturb it as little as possible. The house faces south toward a pond created by the owners, and the structure nestles into the hillside, fitting into the landscape with no exposure to the north. The house's passive-solar design features control the flow of energy through the building by natural means, utilizing energy-conservation principles.

The primary building material is concrete—sandblasted in some areas, faced with stone in others. Oak columns and beams lend a feeling of warmth. These materials are used both inside the house and outside in a harmonious arrangement.

Much consideration was given to the proportion of the walls and the balance of glass areas with the spaces behind them. Natural light spills into the north end of the house via a long row of skylights. Even on an overcast day, one does not feel "underground" in any room. The rich colors of the wood, stone, and other materials further forestall any sense of subterranean space.

Above: *Viewed from the east, the house appears to become part of the site.*

Opposite Page: *From the southeast, the house opens to sunlight under its earth-covered roof.*

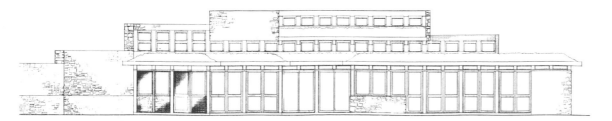

⊕ South

1. Entry
2. Master Bedroom
3. Guest Bedroom
4. Living Room
5. Kitchen
6. Dining Room
7. Studio
8. Porch

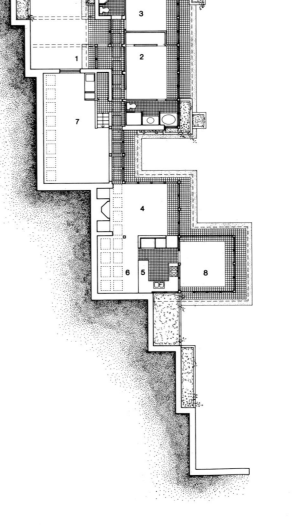

Floor Plan

Opposite Page: *Natural stone retaining walls with wood beams define the entry court and accentuate the living room.*

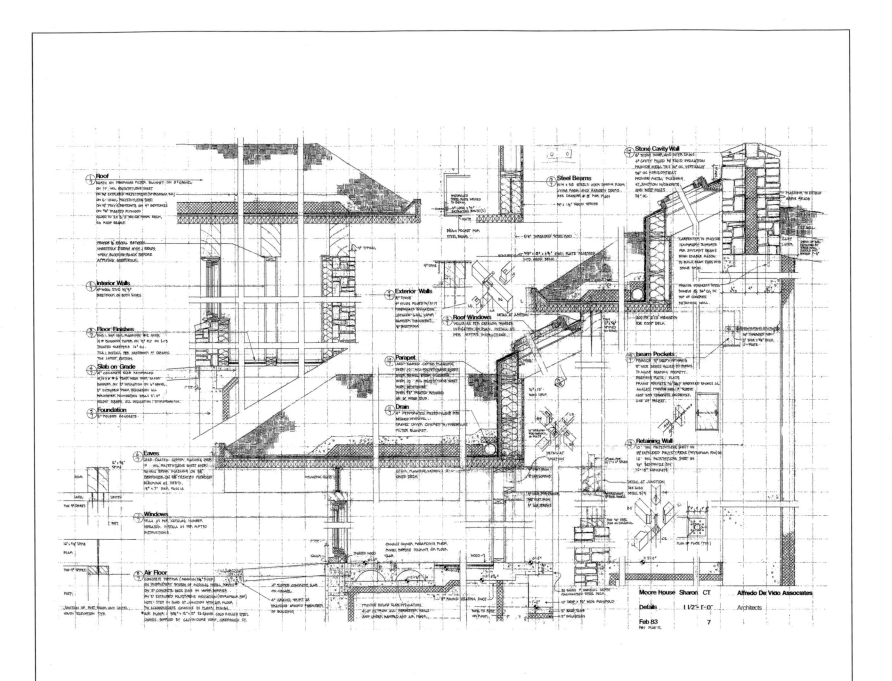

Moore House Sharon CT

Details 1 1/2"=1'-0"

Feb 83 7
Rev Mar 12

Alfredo De Vido Associates

Architects

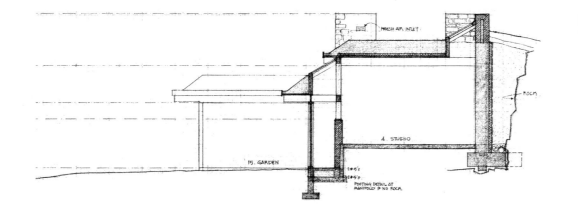

FRESH AIR INLET

ROCK

4. STUDIO

15. GARDEN

1 of 5's
2 of 5's
FOOTING DETAIL AT
MANIFOLD IF NO ROCK.

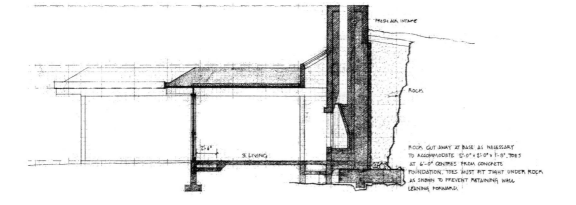

FRESH AIR INTAKE

ROCK

2'-6"

3. LIVING

ROCK CUT AWAY AT BASE AS NECESSARY
TO ACCOMMODATE 2'-0" x 2'-0" x 1'-8". TOES
AT 6'-0" CENTRES FROM CONCRETE
FOUNDATION. TOES MUST FIT TIGHT UNDER ROCK
AS SHOWN TO PREVENT RETAINING WALL
LEANING FORWARD.

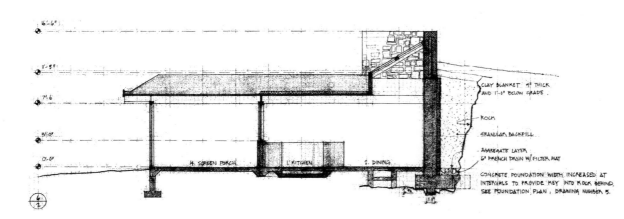

16'-6"

11'-5"

7'-6

3'-0"

0'-0"

14. SCREEN PORCH.   1. KITCHEN   2. DINING

CLAY BLANKET 9" THICK
AND 1'-0" BELOW GRADE.

ROCK

GRANULAR BACKFILL

AGGREGATE LAYER
6" FRENCH DRAIN W/ FILTER MAT

CONCRETE FOUNDATION WIDTH INCREASED AT
INTERVALS TO PROVIDE KEY INTO ROCK BEHIND.
SEE FOUNDATION PLAN, DRAWING NUMBER 5.

House in San Martin

San Martin de los Andes, Neuquen, Argentina
Lacroze Miguens Prati Architects

C antilevered off the Andean mountain face and tucked under a grass-covered, concrete kerchief, this wooden deck—wedged into a crevice—translates the basic physical and spiritual needs of refuge into built form, spelled out by a simple program in a harsh environment.

In an attitude of deliberate self-denial, the shelter turns its back on those who approach it. A parochial shingled turret protrudes from a blanket of grass, the only discernible sign of its existence. Instead, it opens itself onto the abyss beyond. A wood-mullioned curtainwall, angled so as to maximize sun penetration and shade projection, barely demarcates spatial boundaries and defines the one recognizable architectural element in this effacing non-building. Sandwiched between roof shell and floordeck, the "house" lacks any other interior plane of reference. Exposed rock becomes the spatial wrapper.

Towering in center stage, the Russian stove, a wood-fed firebrick source of radiant heat and hot water, becomes the only recognizable orthogonal spatial fulcrum in this otherwise grotto-like structure. Personal needs—bathing, sleeping—are symmetrically sidelined into the roof folds, concealed by floating screens and storage units. Spartan furniture and a few objects sprinkled at random, by their sole presence, transcend utility and become strongly referential.

Above: For all its bravado, the humble shingled entryway, which doubles as a thermal flue, is the only indication of a house's existence to the unaware approaching visitor.

Left: Solidly anchored into the Andean rock, the grass-covered refuge emerges vigilant over the Valley beyond.

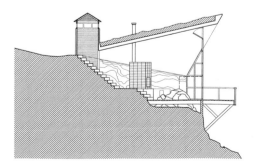

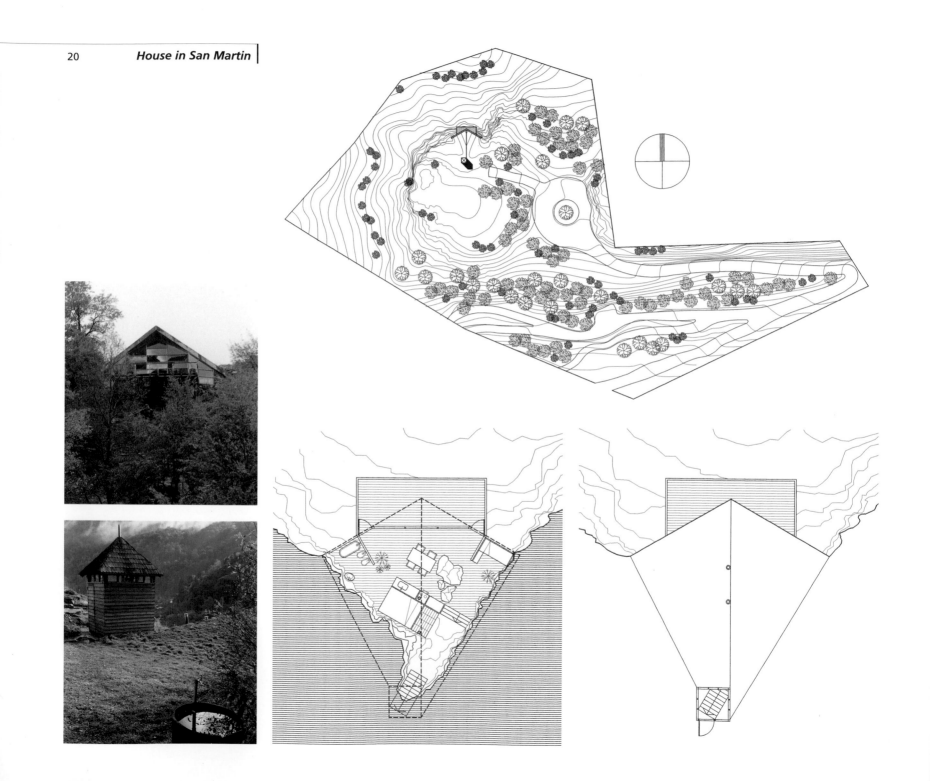

Left: *Simultaneously assertive and submissive, the house's geometry is both emphasized and tamed by nature.*

Opposite Page: *Not unlike an architectural Jekyll and Hyde, the shingled turret is the unassuming counterface of the proudly jutting, sparkling trapeze.*

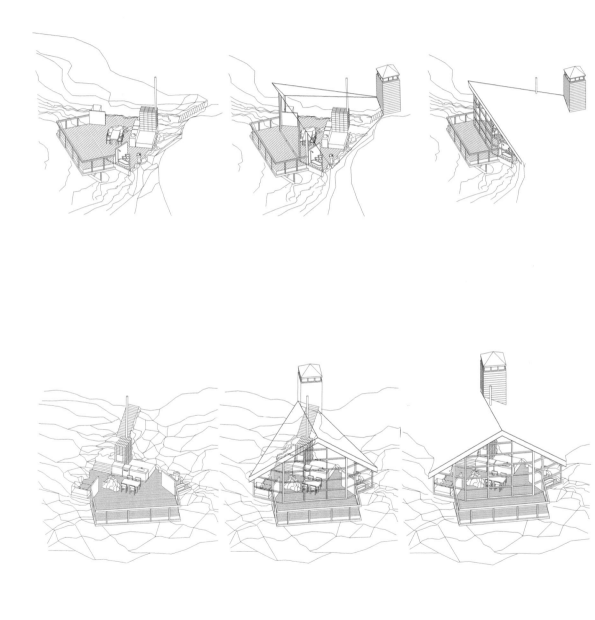

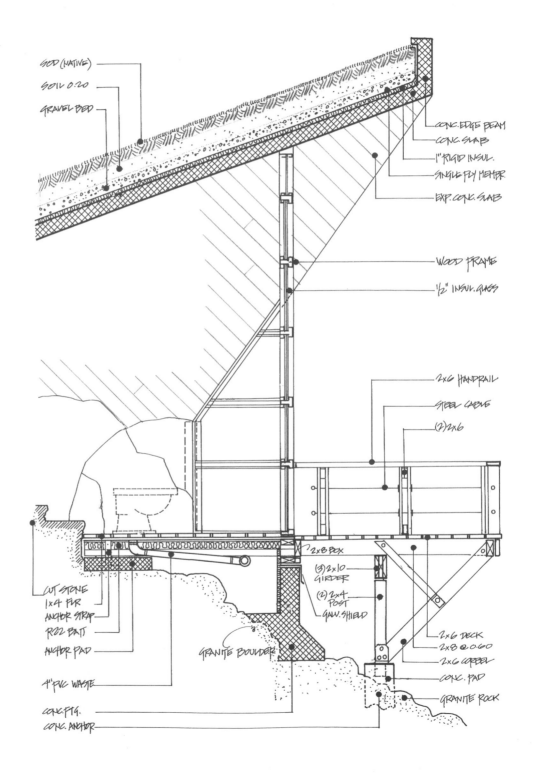

SOD (NATIVE)

SOIL 0:20

GRAVEL BED

CONC. EDGE BEAM
CONC. SLAB
1" RIGID INSUL.
SINGLE PLY MEMBR
EXP. CONC. SLAB

WOOD FRAME

1/2" INSUL. GLASS

2x6 HANDRAIL

STEEL CABLE

(2) 2x6

2x8 BOX

(3) 2x10 GIRDER

(2) 2x4 POST
GALV. SHIELD

CUT STONE
1x4 FLR
ANCHOR STRAP
R22 BATT
ANCHOR PAD

GRANITE BOULDER

4" PVC WASTE

2x6 DECK
2x8 @ 0.60
2x6 CORBEL
CONC. PAD
GRANITE ROCK

CONC. FTG.
CONC. ANCHOR

House in Gorriti Street

Calle Gorriti, Buenos Aires, Argentina
Lacroze Miguens Prati Architects

Confronted with a non-distinctive location—the repetitive, sliver-shaped urban lot—this house constitutes an exploration into reclusive self-containment and spatial implosion. Withdrawing from the featureless surroundings through a blank, pierced front wall that conceals an atrium-like, open courtyard, the house is conceived as a spatial continuum that meanders through a hollowed horizontal prism and is punctuated by service wrappers articulating function areas.

To achieve visual continuity, the service core is totally detached from the load-bearing party walls that penetrate the layering of outdoor/indoor spaces. Axially reverted into a longitudinal parade of decomposed, free-standing elements, the service units become self-expressive. The orthogonal planes are detached from one another, with all intersecting lines dissolved through the use of glass slits that replace the conventional punch-hole fenestration and ensure maximum penetration of light and sight. Individualized and isolated through the use of light and color, a Mondrianesque grid of primary colors reinforces a thoroughly urban and intellectual Kandinskian puzzle of Point, Line, and Plane. Concept, as translated by color with the help of light, becomes the primary expressive vehicle. Self-effacing, quasi-industrial detailing—seamless surfaces, steel girders, and exposed concrete—reinforce the message of choice within a budget.

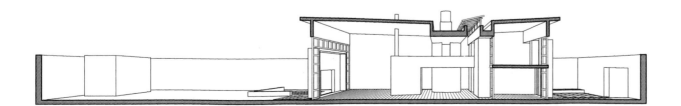

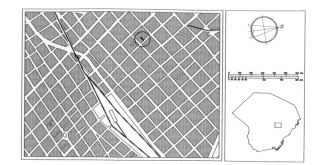

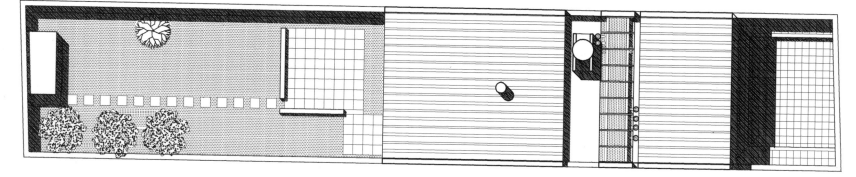

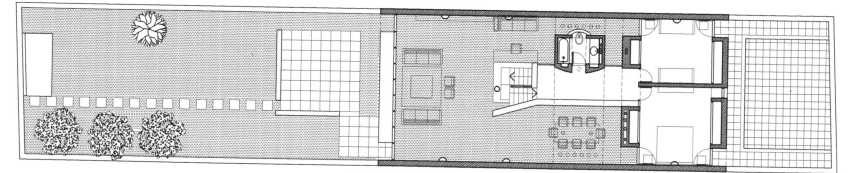

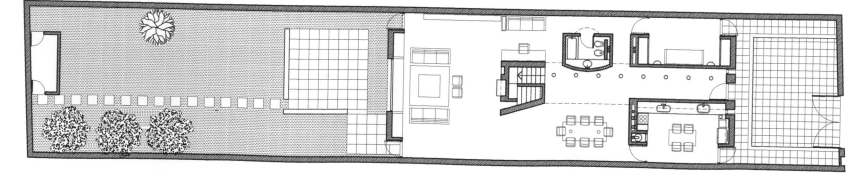

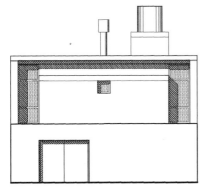

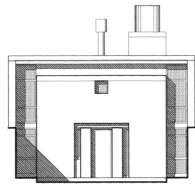

Left: *The modular fenestration, including the wraparound ribbon windows, strictly emphasizes the freestanding quality of the inner sanctum facades, to be understood more as constituent planes of the interior than as enclosure barriers from the exterior.*

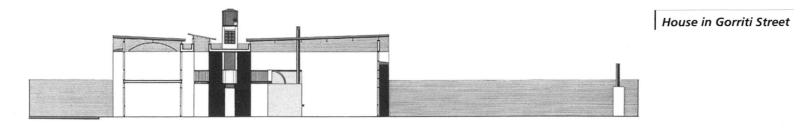

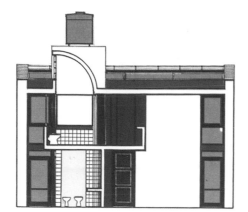

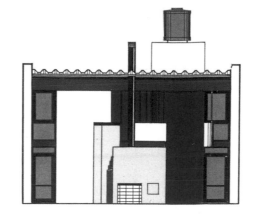

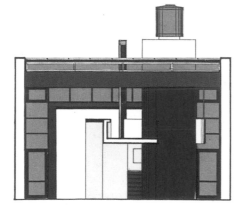

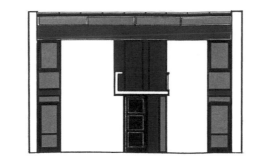

Opposite Page: The service core is decomposed into a Mondrianesque grid of intersecting planes, their primary colors set against the flowing continuum of the confining party walls.

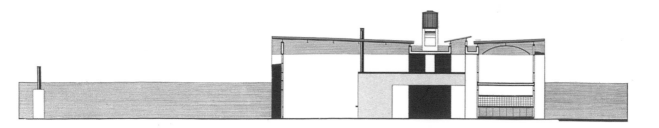

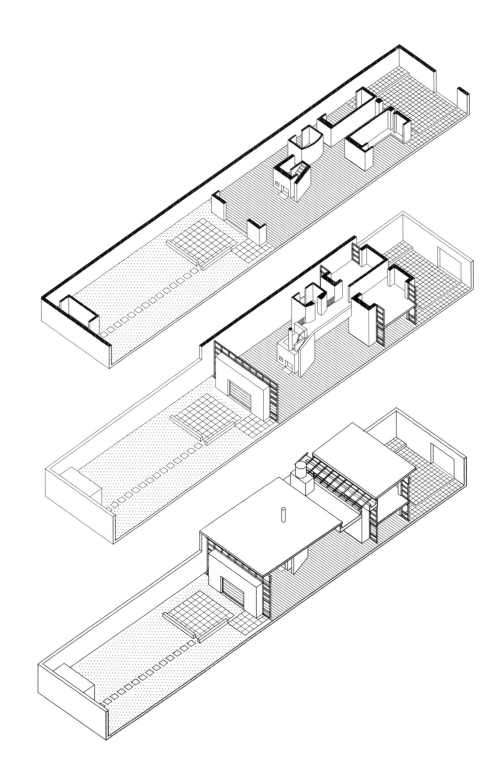

Previous Page and Right: Within the constantly changing vignettes proposed by the ongoing spatial promenade, the distinctive contours of award-winning designer Diana Cabeza's furniture become referential icons. Form, texture and color infuse domesticity into the conceptual rigors of a complexly layered spatial structure.

DET. @ ROOFLINE
1 - GALV. FLUE
2 - FLSHG' COLLAR
3 - GALV. ROOF
4 - SPRAY INSUL. 2"
5 - STEEL GIRDER - PN1 12
6 - MEMBRANE
7 - RIGID INSUL. 1"
8 - CONC. SLAB (EXP.)
9 - EXP. CONC. (BEYOND)
10 - LINE of STUCCO (BYD.)
11 - HALOGEN

DET. @ STAIRWELL
12 - 42" ST. HANDRAIL
13 - BRICK PARAPET
14 - CONC. SLAB (EXP)
15 - 2¼" FIR FLRG.
16 - RADIANT HT. SLAB
17 - STUCCO (BYD.)
18 - ¾" WD. TRD.
19 - CONC. STAIR SLAB
20 - CONC. FTG.
21 - LINE of WBFP (BYD)

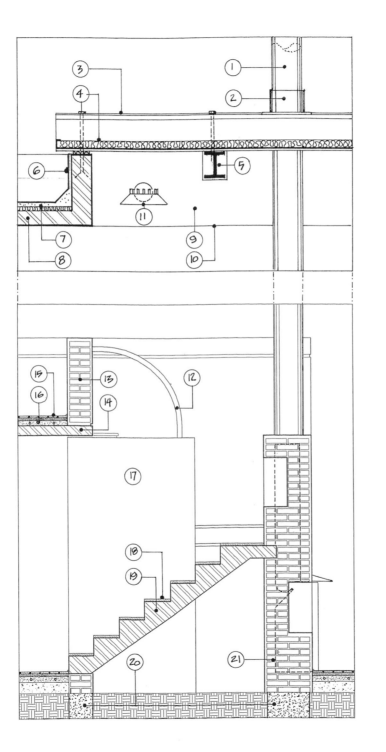

House in Carranza Street

Palermo Viejo, Buenos Aires, Argentina

Lacroze Miguens Prati Architects

S et on a deeper-than-usual urban sliver lot and constructed within the constraints of a tight budget, this house was envisioned as a linear succession of indoor and outdoor spaces designed to meet the needs of a young couple. The resulting program deliberately broke down into two independent living units: house and study/poolhouse.

The house—a glass enclosed cube tucked halfway into the lot and wedged between party walls containing a two-tiered package of cooking and sleeping trays overlooking a hollowed out main void—is resolved conceptually as the interaction of Mondrianesque grids defined by the visual layering of fenestration and planar intersections (walls / floors / ceilings). Deliberately superimposed and underlined by a soft palette that emphasizes the blurring of defined boundaries, the visual layering achieves a degree of perceptive ambiguity. This renders scaleless the compressed space—thus making it boundless. The roughly textured, bow-fronted fireplace emerges as the visual fulcrum of this compressed space.

The pavilion-like study incorporates the pool within its roof terrace, providing a controlled visual backdrop and a functional extension of the rear garden while avoiding blight created by an empty pool during the winter. In contrast, the front yard acts as an overscaled welcome mat: screened by a transitional wall framing the main cubicle in a gesture of uplifting grandeur, its directionality is underlined by a guiding steel curb.

__Above:__ An industrial curtain gate cut into a nondescript wall acts both as screen and gateway, providing anonymity and transition.

__Opposite Page:__ Encased between free-flowing party walls, the gridlike precision of the Albertian facade instills a measure of control to the continuum of the patio.

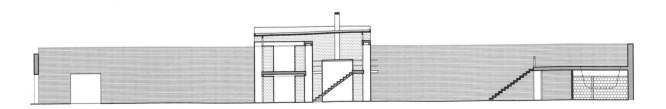

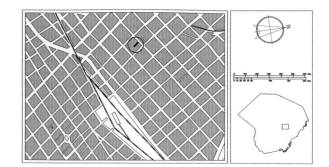

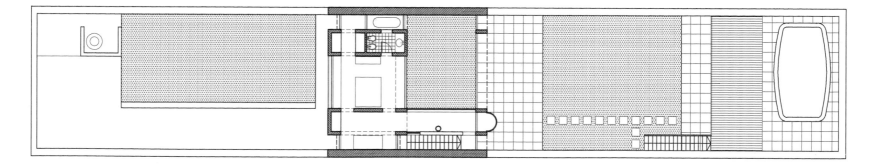

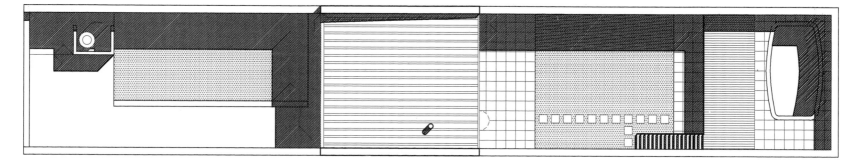

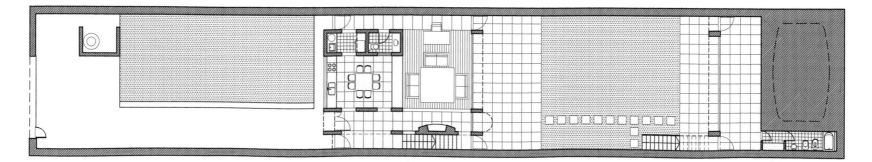

Above: The rigid geometry of the steel-framed glass wall becomes the only reference of an interior-exterior boundary.

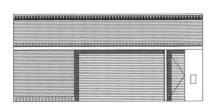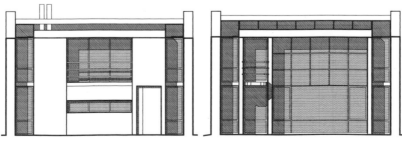

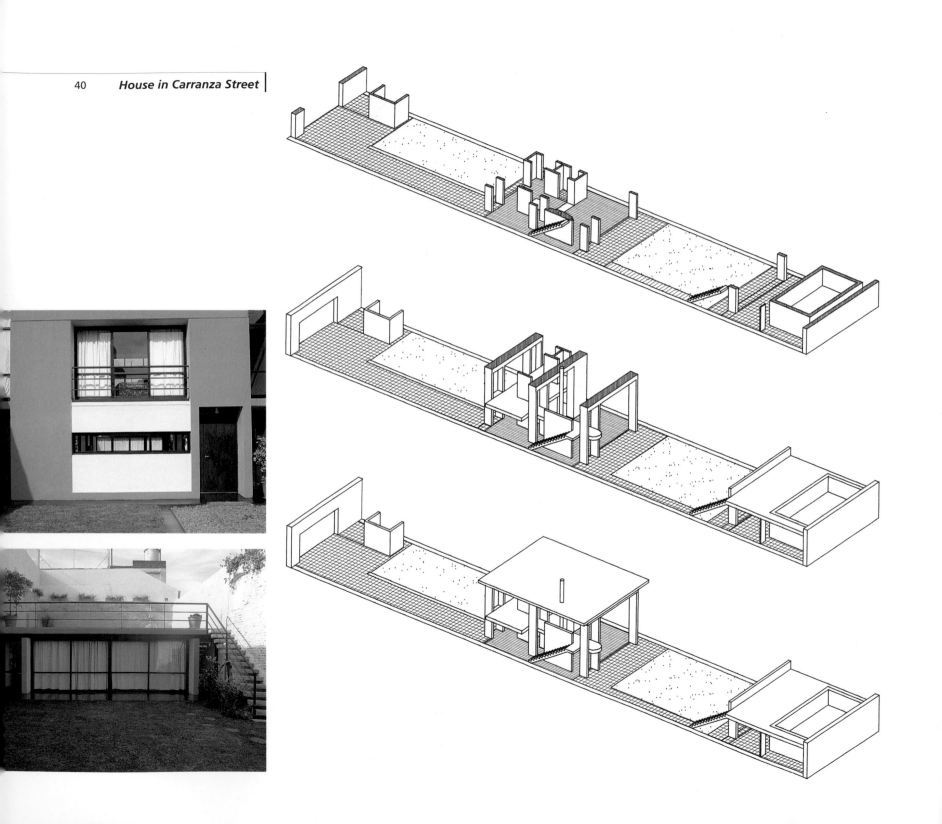

Previous Page and Right: *The coarsely textured brick fireplace and its brightly colored flue boldly pierce through the pastel walls and light-flooded voids, firmly stressing the homely hearth as the house's visual and emotional fulcrum.*

Opposite Page: *The superimposition of referential grids introduces a degree of ambiguity that simultaneously expands and contracts the spatial readings, creating illusory perspectives that enrich the visual experience of the otherwise modest cubicle.*

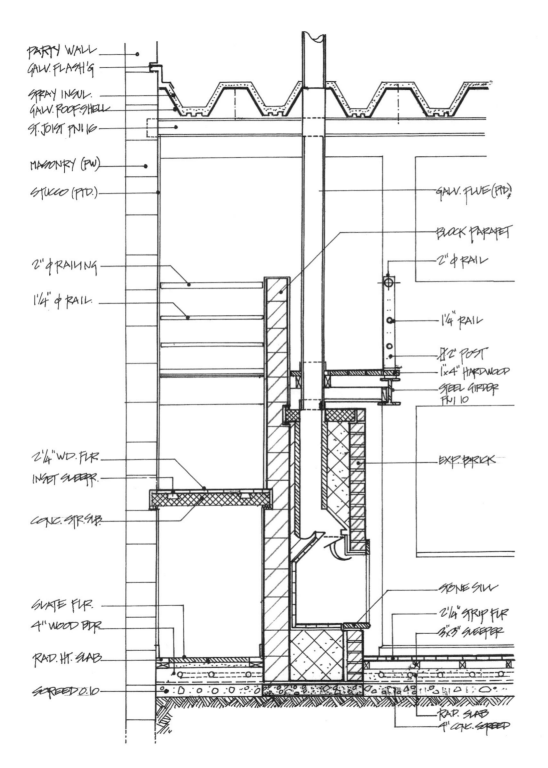

PARTY WALL
GALV. FLASH'G
SPRAY INSUL.
GALV. ROOF SHELL
ST. JOIST PNL 16

MASONRY (PW)
STUCCO (PTD.)

2" Ø RAILING

1¼" Ø RAIL.

2¼" WD. FLR.
INSET SLEEPR.

CONC. STR. SLAB.

SLATE FLR.
4" WOOD BDR
RAD. HT. SLAB.
SCREED 0.10

GALV. FLUE (PTD.)

BLOCK PARAPET
2" Ø RAIL

1¼" RAIL

8½" POST
1"x4" HARDWOOD
STEEL GIRDER
PNL 10

EXP. BRICK

STONE SILL
2¼" STRIP FLR.
3"x3" SLEEPER

RAD. SLAB
4" CONC. SCREED

House on Paul Harris Street

Las Condes, Santiago, Chile
Enrique Browne Architects

Above: *From the street, only the creeper-covered pergola is visible.*

Opposite Page: *View of the house from the back garden.*

The 89-by-257-foot (27-by-78-meter) lot is located in the eastern part of Santiago, oriented on the north-south axis. There are large pine trees at the back of the property, and the Andes Mountains can be seen to the east. The house is located at the center of the lot in order to maximize the views surrounding the lot. Designed on two levels, the first level of the house is for public spaces, the second for private.

Dividing walls border the lot, as the location of the house created two open zones to the south and the north. The north end of the lot also is divided in half by an entrance parrón. Three patios were thus formed: an entrance patio, a front patio, and a patio-garden to the south. The house was developed from a tall and elongated central space, reconciled by two parallel wall-beams. This space vents sun to the southern areas of the house and concentrates horizontal and vertical circulation. The covering is made of thermopanes to avoid heat loss. An undulating lower wall provides a counterpoint to the geometric rigidity of the wall-beams. This contemporary version of the central patio serves as a nucleus for the whole composition. Similarly, two roofs and two pergolas adhere with an inverted geometry on both sides.

The closure of the house is independent of the described volumes. It consists of a continuous line of glass that zigzags freely between the walls and the pillars, forming two diverse internal and intermediate spaces. The house thus acquires layers, leaving "spaces within spaces." The interior-exterior gradation also is expressed in the plasticity of the house. The intermediate spaces are the most figurative. They have controlled vegetation, red tones of wood in the ceilings, and brick in the flooring. Outside, the green of the trees and the colors of the mountains are the noticeable elements. This play between figure and abstraction is evident in the elevations: the frontal facades tend toward the figure, while the lateral facades tend toward abstraction.

paul harris street

SITE PLAN
1. Entrance Patio
2. Garden Patio
3. Pool

FIRST FLOOR PLAN
1. Entrance Hall
2. Dining Room
3. Living Room
4. Kitchen
5. Service Bedroom
6. Laundry
7. Pergola
8. Office-Bedroom

SECOND FLOOR PLAN
9. Bedrooms
10. Studio
11. Children's Study
12. Terrace

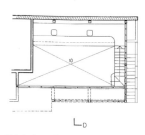

Third Floor Plan

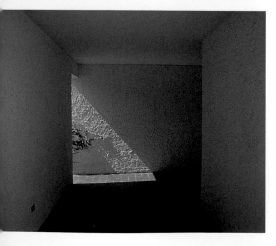

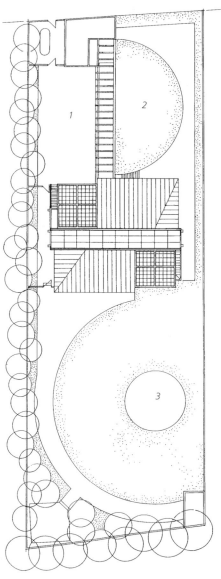

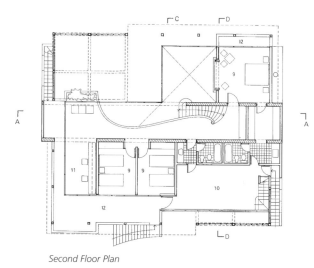

Second Floor Plan

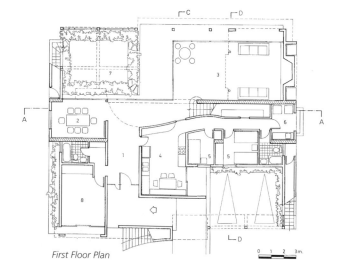

First Floor Plan

0 1 2 3m.

Left: *A creeper plant—whose leaves turn red and yellow in autumn—covers the pergola.*

Opposite Page: *(Top) Trellised entrance to the house. (Bottom) To enter the dwelling, one needs to make a double turn, passing through this minimal space.*

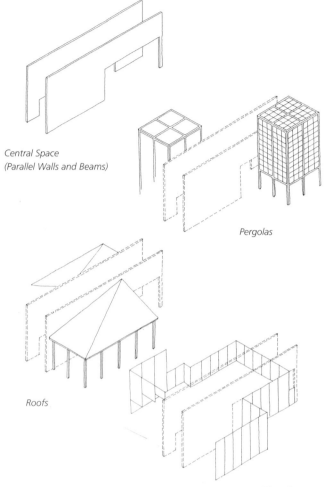

Central Space
(Parallel Walls and Beams)

Pergolas

Roofs

Glass Contour

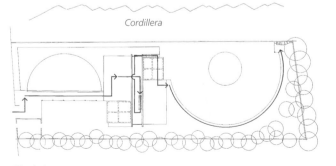

Cordillera

Circulation

Left: *(Top) The western and eastern sides of the house, which face toward the neighbors, are closed off. (Center) This stairway leads from the central corridor toward the garden pergola. (Bottom) The partition between interior and exterior spaces is achieved by a crystal membrane, which winds between ceilings and pergolas. As such, the partition is notably discreet in appearance.*

Opposite Page: *The front-facing pergola shields a window-lined, informal living room.*

Right: (Top) View of the living room and the main bedroom. The stairway to the first floor is on the right. (Bottom) Views of the glass-roofed main hallway.

Opposite Page: The outer curve of the corridor passes through the glass partition, entering into the pergola.

The different spatial situations can be appreciated by an "architectonic walk," which begins in the main entrance door and ends at a pergola with a fountain at the rear of the grounds. Because of its inverted geometry, the house seems to turn round as the walker advances.

The pergolas and the other intermediate spaces increase the volume of the house. The proportions of the plans and the elevations are accomplished both in the house and in the exteriors. A 10-foot (3-meter) module was adopted for such effects.

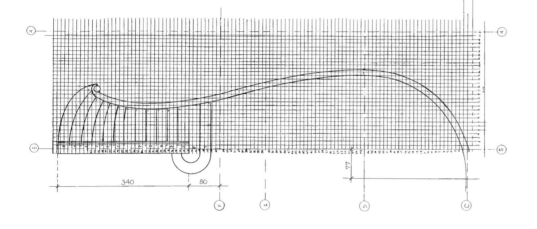

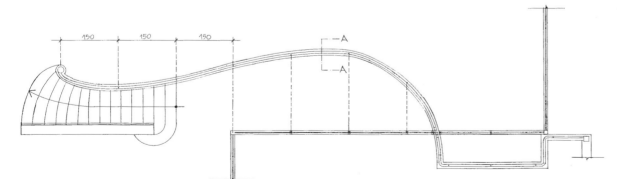

Handrail and Staircase Outline

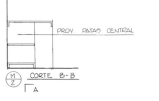

PROY. PATAS CENTRAL

(M/2) CORTE B-B

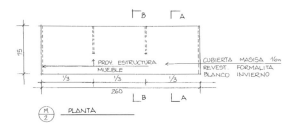

CUBIERTA MASISA 16n
REVEST. FORMALITA
BLANCO INVIERNO

¹/₃   ¹/₃   ¹/₃

260

(M/2) PLANTA

75
45   30   FONDO MURO

CUBIERTA Y DIVISIONES
MASISA 16 mm REVEST.
FORMALITA BLANCA.

PROY. PATAS LATERALES

D2

(M/2) CORTE A-A

CUBIERTA MASISA 16mm.

REVEST. FORMALITA BLANCA
ARISTA A 45°

BORDE ALAMO 1"×2" CEP.

FRENTE CAJON EUCALIPTUS
1" × 4" ELABORADO
PROYECCION SACADO
RADIO = 4 CMS.

FONDO CAJON
TERCIADO 6mm.

D1

CUBIERTA MASISA 16mm
REVEST. FORMALITA BLANCA ARISTA 45°

BORDE ALAMO 1" × 3" CEP.

D2

Studio Furniture Details

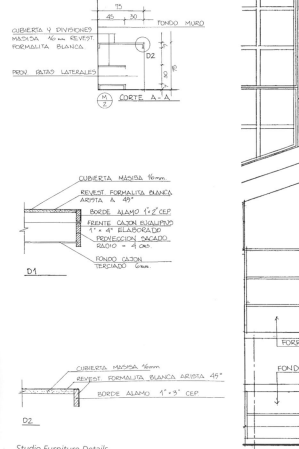
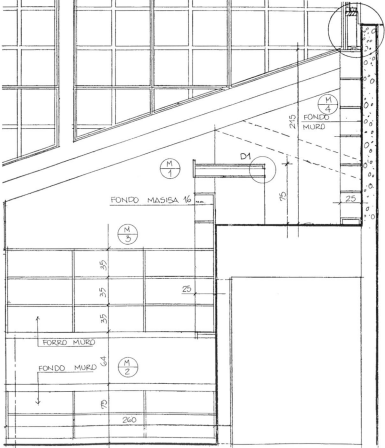

FONDO
MURO

215

D1

75

FONDO MASISA 16 mm.

25

(M/3)

35

35   25

35

FORRO MURO

FONDO MURO   64

(M/2)

75

260

Snail House

Las Condes, Santiago, Chile
Enrique Browne Architects

The essence of patios forms the basis for the design of this house. The owners sought a dwelling that would form an indissoluble unity with the terrain. The house would not "be in" the site; rather, it would "be" the site. For this reason, the construction of the dividing wall between the Snail House and its neighbors was the first architectonic decision.

The site was almost square. The best views and sunlight were on the northern diagonal toward the street. This diagonal became the axis of the whole composition. The common areas (dining room and living room) were separated from the private spaces (bedrooms and service areas) and located in the center of the terrain, forming their own site. It started as a more compact form: a circle. Upon adjusting this space on the diagonal, an oval was formed. Given that the dining room and kitchen do not require bathrooms, the oval was left at the height of the natural terrain, 4 feet (1.2 meters).

The detached private areas (parents' bedroom, children's bedroom, and service areas) are located between the oval and the square of the dividing wall. These units form small patios and are left at street level, so as to connect bathrooms and kitchens to the public services (water and sewage).

Conceptually unifying the different parts of the house was an important part of the program. A spiral circulating around the oval achieved that unifying essence. The wall that forms the spiral begins in the entranceway and ends in a waterfall over the pool. Certain technical items, including the stairs to the roof, the boiler, and television and radio antennas are concentrated in a metallic tower on the back patio and over the axis in diagonal.

The house is white but it is painted with natural overhead light. In the gallery, the light is white, while in the dining room (the symbolic nucleus), it is yellow. There is a cut in the roof that illuminates the covered terrace beside the living room with blue light.

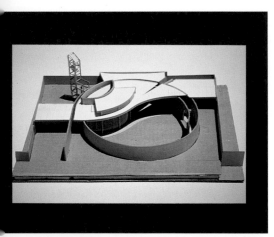

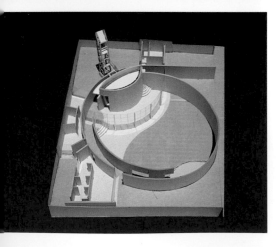

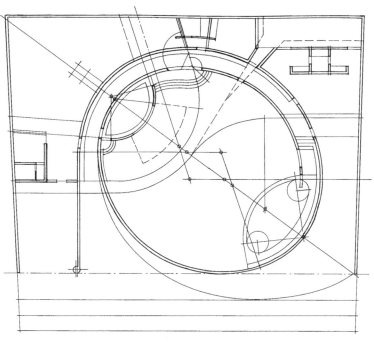

Geometry

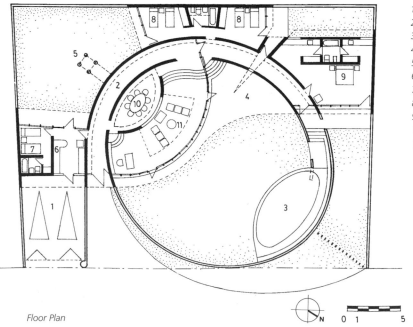

Floor Plan

1. Parking
2. Gallery
3. Pool
4. Covered Terrace
5. Mechanical Tower
6. Kitchen
7. Service Quarters
8. Bedroom
9. Parents' Bedroom
10. Dining Room
11. Living Room

0   1   5

Right: (Top) Daytime view of the patio-garden, seen from the covered terrace. (Bottom) Views of water falling into the pool.

Opposite Page: (Top) View of the house from the pool. (Bottom) Covered terrace.

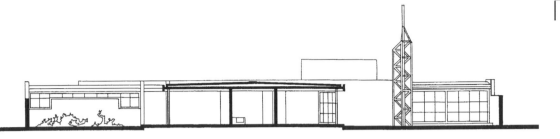

Longitudinal Section

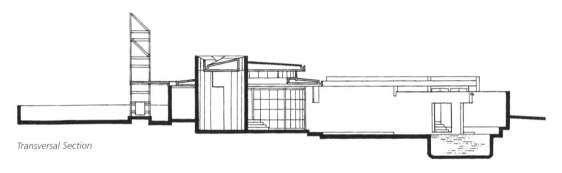

Transversal Section

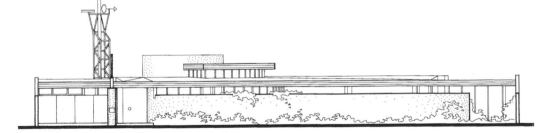

Street Elevation

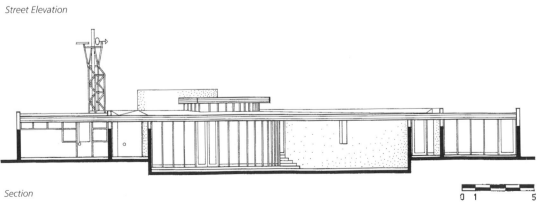

Section

0 1 5

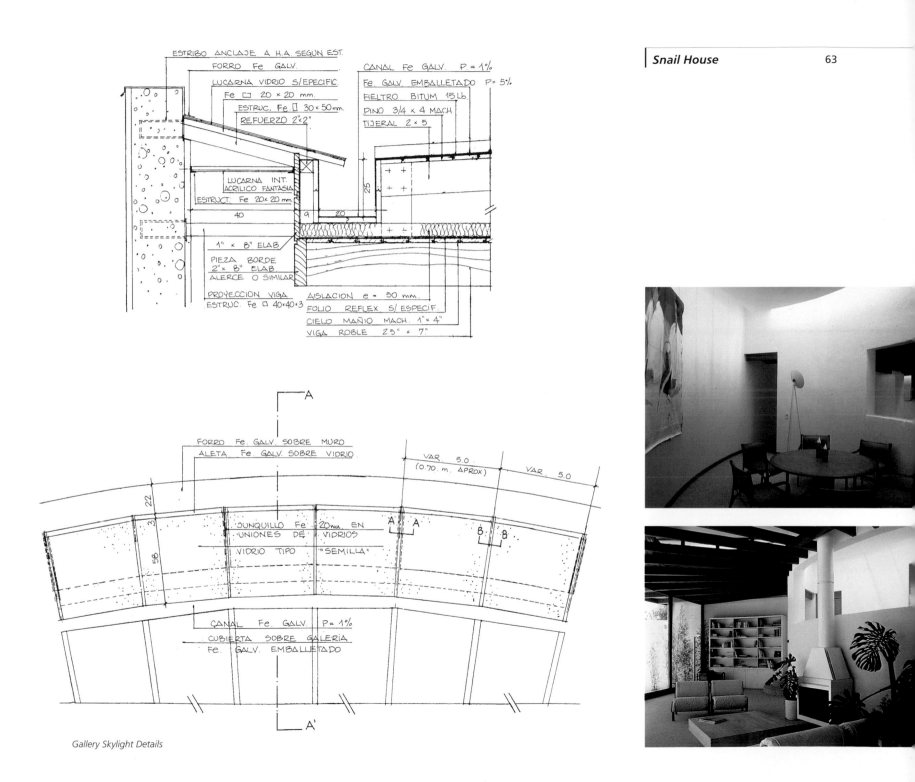

ESTRIBO ANCLAJE A H.A. SEGUN EST.

FORRO Fe GALV.

LUCARNA VIDRIO S/EPECIFIC.

Fe ☐ 20 × 20 mm.

ESTRUC. Fe ☐ 30 × 50 mm.

REFUERZO 2"×2"

CANAL Fe GALV. P = 1%

Fe GALV. EMBALLETADO P = 5%

FIELTRO BITUM 15 Lb.

PINO 3/4 × 4 MACH

TIJERAL 2 × 5

LUCARNA INT.
ACRILICO FANTASIA

ESTRUCT. Fe 20 × 20 mm.

25

40   9   20

1" × 8" ELAB

PIEZA BORDE
2" × 8" ELAB.
ALERCE O SIMILAR

PROYECCION VIGA
ESTRUC. Fe ☐ 40 × 40 × 3

AISLACION e = 50 mm.

FOLIO REFLEX. S/ESPECIF.

CIELO MAÑIO MACH. 1" × 4"

VIGA ROBLE 2.5" × 7"

A

FORRO Fe. GALV. SOBRE MURO

ALETA Fe. GALV. SOBRE VIDRIO

VAR. 5.0.
(0.70. m. APROX)

VAR. 5.0

22

3

58

JUNQUILLO Fe 20mm. EN
UNIONES DE VIDRIOS

VIDRIO TIPO "SEMILLA"

A   A

B   B

CANAL Fe. GALV. P = 1%

CUBIERTA SOBRE GALERIA
Fe. GALV. EMBALLETADO

A'

Gallery Skylight Details

Garcia House

Santiago, Chile

Christian De Groote Architects

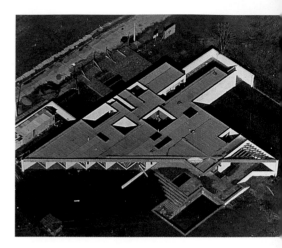

L ocated in Las Condes, this 43,000 square-foot (4,000-square-meter) site ended up rather small for developing this very ambitious program that included a tennis court that, by itself, required a fifth of the available area. At the client's request, the house included a study connected to the master bedroom that also faces an inner patio, giving the study total privacy. This requirement allowed us to make a quite dense ground plan.

As the axis of the view toward the Andes mountains follows a forty-five-degree deviation in relation to the site, we placed the tennis court close to a corner and the house against it, laying out the site on a large diagonal and forming two triangles. The house and the tennis court occupy one of these triangles, and the garden occupies the other. This produces the impression of an open area much larger than it really is, while giving the house a long front facing the mountains.

The dense and compact form established by the equilateral triangle becomes lighter with the creation of inner patios, which articulate the ground plan and define the different areas of the program. The exterior is treated with painted rough stucco, and the interior is completely lined with honey-colored raw silk paneling, lending the house unity and continuity. The only element that differs is the great exposed concrete beam crowning the diagonal of the house, emphasizing its large dimension.

Above: Aerial view of the house, still under construction, showing how the inner patios shape an orthogonal plan without interfering with the large diagonal toward the garden.

Opposite Page: An orthogonal plane that enlarges the area of terraces near the swimming pool intercepts the long diagonal concrete beam.

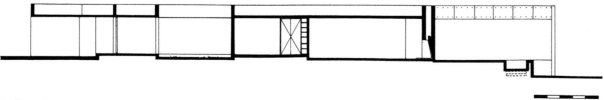

Section A-A

0   5m

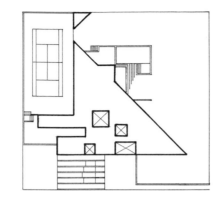

Site Plan

A

1. Entrance
2. Carport
3. Entrance Hall
4. Interior Garden
5. Studio
6. Living Room
7. Dining Room
8. Kitchen
9. Laundry
10. Service Room
11. Mechanical
12. Tennis Court
13. Pool
14. Terrace
15. Master Bedroom
16. Bedroom
17. Family Room
18. Dressing Room
19. Service Yard

Floor Plan

0   5   10   15   20m

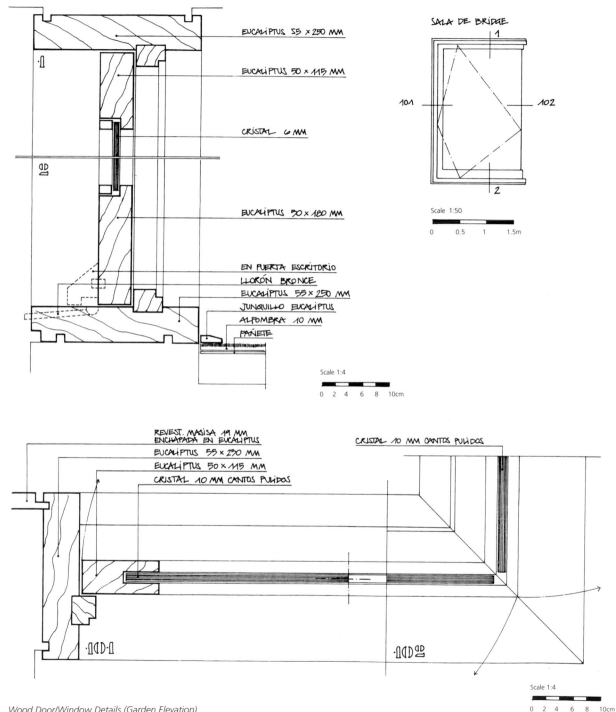

EUCALIPTUS 55 × 250 MM

EUCALIPTUS 50 × 115 MM

CRISTAL 6 MM

EUCALIPTUS 50 × 180 MM

EN PUERTA ESCRITORIO
LLORÓN BRONCE
EUCALIPTUS 55 × 250 MM
JUNQUILLO EUCALIPTUS
ALFOMBRA 10 MM
PAÑETE

Scale 1:4

0　2　4　6　8　10cm

SALA DE BRIDGE

1

101　　102

2

Scale 1:50

0　0.5　1　1.5m

REVEST. MASISA 19 MM
ENCHAPADA EN EUCALIPTUS
EUCALIPTUS 55 × 250 MM
EUCALIPTUS 50 × 115 MM
CRISTAL 10 MM CANTOS PULIDOS

CRISTAL 10 MM CANTOS PULIDOS

Scale 1:4

0　2　4　6　8　10cm

Wood Door/Window Details (Garden Elevation)

Constanza Vergara House

Algarrobo, Chile

Christian De Groote Architects

A sea resort on the Pacific, Algarrobo lies approximately 75 miles (120 kilometers) to the southwest of Santiago. This house is located at the northern end of the town, Algarrobo's oldest and most urban area. The site, very small in size—approximately 4,750 square feet (440 square meters)—is set directly in front of the beach about seven feet (two meters) above the sand.

Conceived as a totally blind back, the street façade consists of a completely blank stone wall in keeping with the character of the neighboring houses. Developed on different planes, the façade produces a sort of bow that marks the beginning of the resort's urban area. The side facing the sea comprises wood and glass, somehow relating the house to the light and graceful architecture of the yachts that sail Algarrobo's small bay. This façade is broken with regard to the orthogonal system of the house structure, in order to face the living room toward the best view and to stress the idea of the house as the end of the urban complex.

Both inside and outside the house, white and black ceramic floor tiling resembles a chess board and enhances the feeling of leisure and ease. At the sight level of a person sitting inside the house or on the terrace, there is only sea to contemplate, such as when sailing. On the other hand, the view from the master bedroom on the second floor, with its large floor-to-ceiling windows, becomes dramatic with the to-and-fro of the waves. All the wood employed, both in the structure and in the covering, is Oregon pine with a honey varnish that lends the house a warm quality.

Above: The volume in wood, corresponding to the master bedroom, shows over the stone wall toward the street. A beautiful tree acts as a natural canopy at the entrance.

Opposite: The rhythm of the windows clearly registers the structure of the wooden posts and beams.

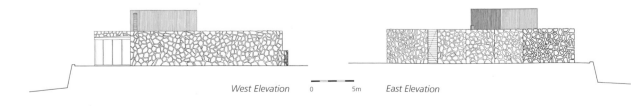

West Elevation   0   5m   East Elevation

Site Plan

First Floor Plan

Second Floor Plan

1. Entrance
2. Parking
3. Service Entrance
4. Service Patio
5. Living Room
6. Dining Room
7. Kitchen
8. Service Bedroom
9. Children Bedroom
10. Guest Bedroom
11. Terrace
12. Garden Patio
13. Beach
14. Master Bedroom
15. Void

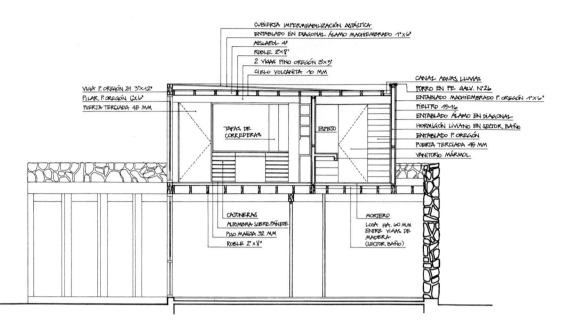

CUBIERTA IMPERMEABILIZACIÓN ASFÁLTICA
ENTABLADO EN DIAGONAL ÁLAMO MACHIEMBRADO 1"x6"
AISLAPOL 4"
ROBLE 2"x8"
2 VIGAS PINO OREGÓN 3"x5"
CIELO VOLCANITA 10 MM

CANAL AGUAS LLUVIAS
FORRO EN FE GALV. N°26
ENTABLADO MACHIEMBRADO P. OREGÓN 1"x6"
FIELTRO 15-16
ENTABLADO ÁLAMO EN DIAGONAL
HORMIGÓN LIVIANO EN SECTOR BAÑO
ENTABLADO P. OREGÓN
PUERTA TERCIADA 45 MM
VANITORIO MÁRMOL

VIGA P. OREGÓN 21 3"x12"
PILAR P. OREGÓN 6x6"
PUERTA TERCIADA 45 MM

TAPAS DE
CORREDERAS

ESPEJO

CAJONERAS
ALFOMBRA SOBRE PAÑETE
PISO MAESA 32 MM
ROBLE 2"x8"

MORTERO
LOSA HA. 60 MM
ENTRE VIGAS DE
MADERA
(SECTOR BAÑO)

Section B-B

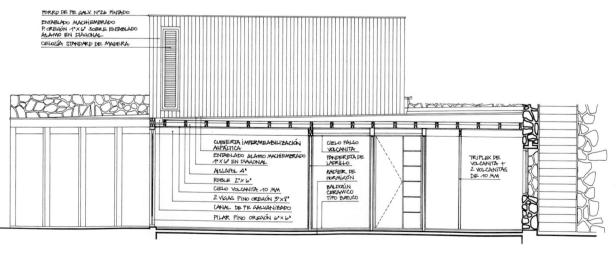

FORRO DE FE GALV. N°26 PINTADO
ENTABLADO MACHIEMBRADO
P. OREGÓN 1"x6" SOBRE ENTABLADO
ÁLAMO EN DIAGONAL
CELOSÍA STANDARD DE MADERA

CUBIERTA IMPERMEABILIZACIÓN
ASFÁLTICA
ENTABLADO ÁLAMO MACHIEMBRADO
1"x6" EN DIAGONAL
AISLAPOL 4"
ROBLE 2"x6"
CIELO VOLCANITA 10 MM
2 VIGAS PINO OREGÓN 3"x8"
CANAL DE FE GALVANIZADO
PILAR PINO OREGÓN 6"x6"

CIELO FALSO
VOLCANITA
PANDERETA DE
LADRILLO
RADIER DE
HORMIGÓN
BALDOSÍN
CERÁMICO
TIPO BATUCO

TRIPLEX DE
VOLCANITA +
2 VOLCANITAS
DE 10 MM

Section A-A

0   1   2m

Matte House

Zapallar, Chile

Christian De Groote Architects

Set on a beautiful spot in a seaside resort, above a fishing cove on the western end of Zapallar Beach, the site was part of the garden and access to the beach of an old manor demolished after the 1970 earthquake. Apart from broken and profuse vegetation, and gigantic old pine trees, the site also had an infrastructure of terraces, walls, and ramps. A turret perched on a large rock served as a lookout tower toward the bay and the beach. All of these structures were constructed out in the typical stone used in the old buildings of the resort.

One of the first basic decisions taken as part of the architectural proposition was the incorporation of the entire infrastructure of walls, terraces, ramps, and turret into the new project. Thus the house would reveal the place and the landscape in the same way it revealed them to the architect the first time he had visited it. The melding of the new constructions and the old remains allowed the project to be embedded in time, dissolving into the landscape as a ruin would.

The project proposed a geography of three low, thick turrets echoing the broken, abrupt anatomy of the Chilean coast. A group of slender towers thrust upward into the air contrasts with trunks of the huge pine trees that are an essential characteristic of the site. These towers established a rhythm defining the elements of the program. The living areas are arranged in platforms resting on the towers and thrown out into space like tree branches. The juxtaposition of only two materials, stone and glass, makes for an unencumbered and austere building that continues, intertwines, and reflects the topography and vegetation of the area.

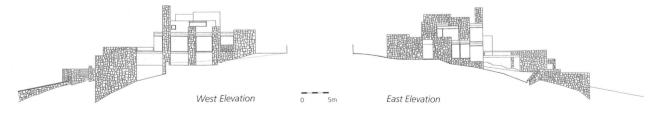

West Elevation   0   5m   *East Elevation*

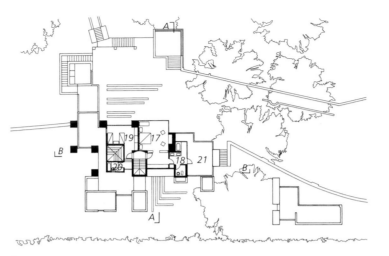

First Floor Plan

1. Entrance
2. Living Room
3. Dining Room
4. Family Living Room
5. Bedroom
6. Bathroom
7. Kitchen
8. Laundry
9. Service Bedroom
10. Mechanical
11. Barbecue Tower
12. Swimming Pool
13. Butler's Living Room/Kitchen
14. Butler's Main Bedroom
15. Butler's Bedroom
16. Butler's Bathroom
17. Master Bedroom
18. Bathroom
19. Guest Bedroom
20. Guest Bathroom
21. Terrace

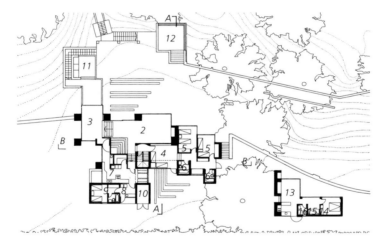

Second Floor Plan

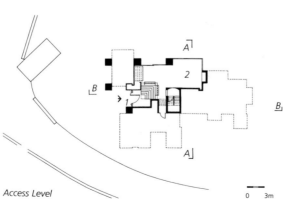

Access Level

0   3m

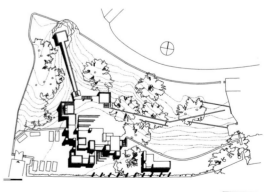

Site Plan

0   15m

This Page: The house camouflages itself with the splendidly wooded landscape, while the stones and towers assert its presence.

Opposite Page: The ground plans clearly show the adaptation of the architecture to the turrets and walls-vestiges, just as to the trees covering the place.

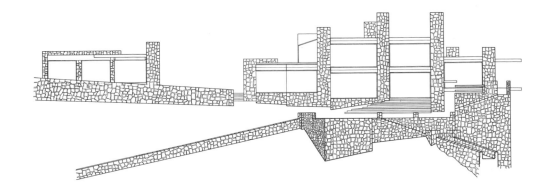

North Elevation

Axonometric View

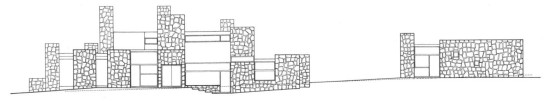

South Elevation

0   5m

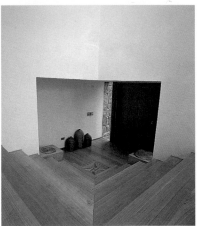

Orrego House

El Pangue, Chile

Christian De Groote Architects

L ocated on a beautiful spot at the seashore, the house lies halfway between the traditional beach resorts of Zapallar and Cachagua, and faces "El Pangue," a marvelous rocky bay. The site, of about 54,000 square feet (5,000 square meters), is set on a hillside between the new and old roads linking the seaside resorts.

Towards the south, halfway between the site and the sea, there is a screen of huge eucalyptus, filtering the view across to the sea and rocks and turning the sunset into a magic sight. The owners, a very sensitive couple, wanted the house to be a true turning point in their lives, and they were placing high hopes in the enterprise, to the extent of describing it as "The Maison Sourire."

The architectural stance establishes a geographical counterpoint with the filter-like screen of eucalyptus, resulting in a linear nature. Moreover, it provides the house total privacy, isolating it from the noise coming from the road running along the upper side of the site.

To achieve this effect, an actual "street" seven feet (two meters) wide was created. Formed by a double wall connecting all the rooms—and acting as an acoustic and visual barrier against the pollution from the road—this street is open to the sky, roofed with double-sealed glass. Along the "street," different rooms form a "town," with intermediate open spaces resembling small squares for relaxation and meditation.

Above: *The long street, forming the spine of the house and constituting the connecting element of the whole, ends on the south in a turret, which dramatizes the descent to the site.*

Opposite Page: *General view of the variety of volumes forming the house, bound together by the contrasting linear street.*

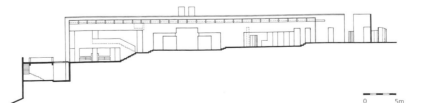

Section A-A

0   5m

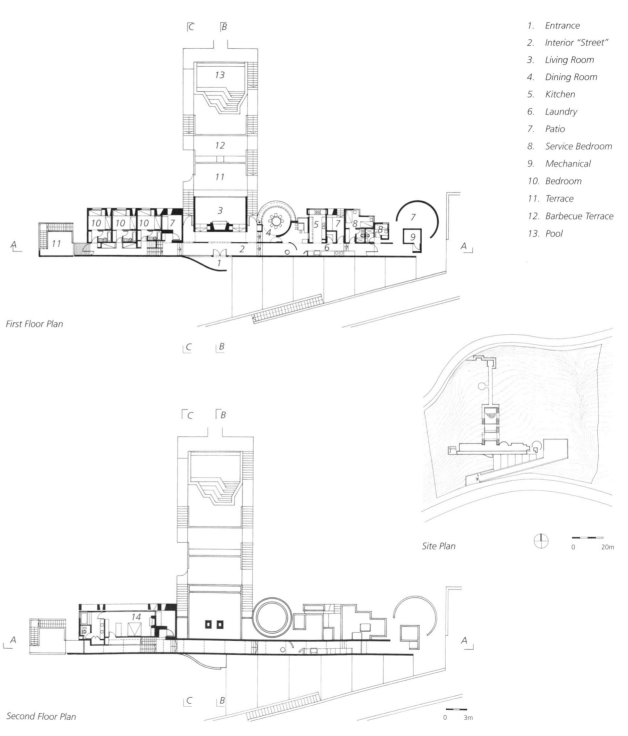

First Floor Plan

Second Floor Plan

1.   Entrance
2.   Interior "Street"
3.   Living Room
4.   Dining Room
5.   Kitchen
6.   Laundry
7.   Patio
8.   Service Bedroom
9.   Mechanical
10. Bedroom
11. Terrace
12. Barbecue Terrace
13. Pool

Site Plan

0   20m

0   3m

This Page: *The three lower photographs show the street with its different levels. The skylight structure also serves the purpose of stabilizing the walls laterally.*

Opposite Page: *The system of terraces and swimming pool, laid out perpendicular to the house, is also the element that connects the upper and lower roads flanking the site.*

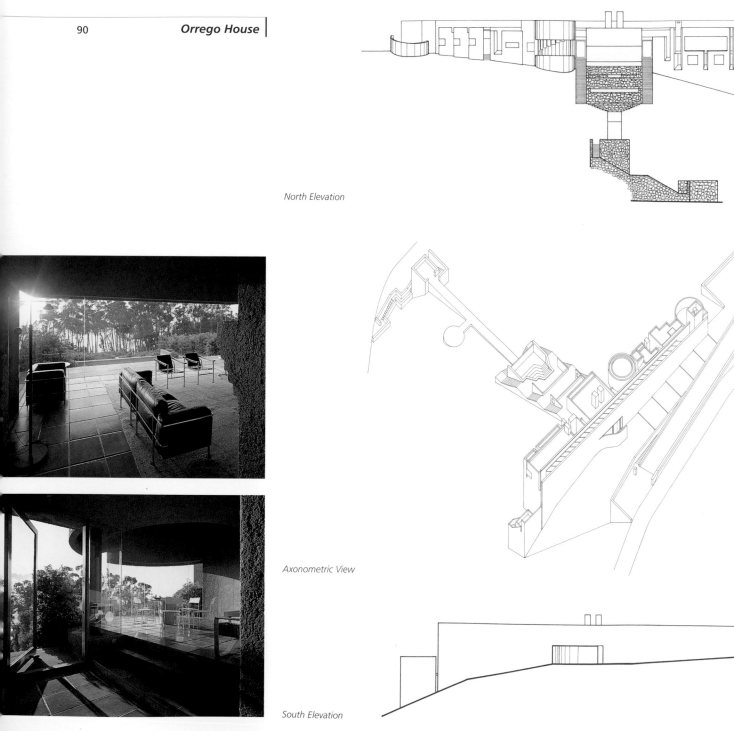

North Elevation

Axonometric View

South Elevation

0   5m

This Page: *The master bedroom's upper photograph, dominates the view toward the ocean through a screen of eucalyptus. Sunset behind this filter becomes a magic sight.*

Opposite Page: *The impenetrability of the house with regard to the road contrasts with the openness of its volumes and terraces toward the sea.*

Elisa House

Santiago, Chile

Christian De Groote Architects

The site, 54,000 square feet (5,000 square meters) in area and located at the feet of the Manquehue Hill, is sharply inclined toward the east and is densely covered with native Chilean trees, especially quillayes, litres, and espinos. The view toward the hills and to the Andes range of mountains—at an angle of practically 180 degrees—is spectacular.

The characteristics of the topography, the vegetation, the surrounding views, and the requirement of providing the house with an heliport led us to the general scheme of building three large "trays" of exposed concrete supported by parallel, stone-covered buttress walls. They make the house "stand on tiptoe" on the slope without changing the natural ground level of the existing trees. These "trays," arranged according to the direction of the contour lines, and the walls, perpendicular to them, are cut out to allow the trees to pierce and determine the perimeter of the house. Thus the tallest and leafiest quillay in the site goes through the interior of the reception area, forming a patio totally surrounded by glass, which in turn allows a spatial interconnection among the different levels. The interior spaces are delimited by large panes of glass with no visible frames, allowing a spectacular and uninterrupted view of the mountains and surrounding vegetation.

In order to enhance the importance of this building and, at the same time, to closely bind the "trays" to the topography, a greenhouse surrounded by a ramp was built to the south. To the east, a system of wide ramps connect the three main levels of the house and those of the garden and terraces.

Above: *Aerial view of the house showing the painstaking adaptation to the site's topography and native vegetation.*

Opposite Page: *Out of consideration for the topography, the garden comprises a geography of steps that slips under the house to surface at the back.*

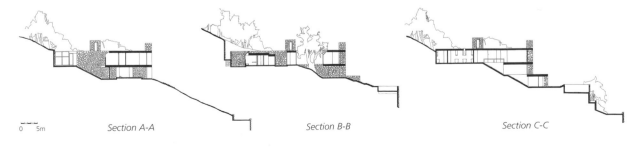

0   5m

Section A-A   *Section B-B*   *Section C-C*

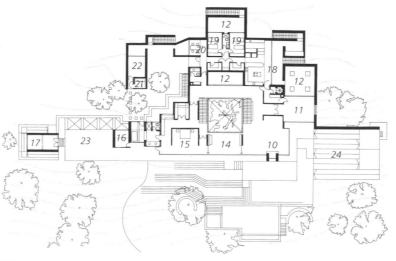

Main Level

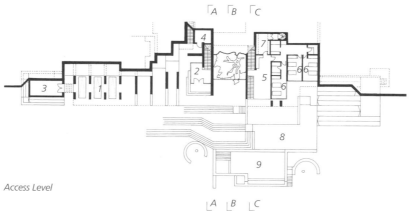

Access Level

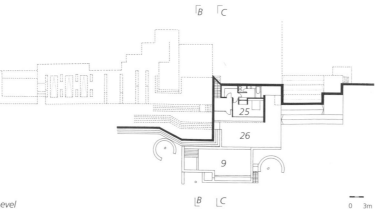

Lower Level

0   3m

Site Plan

0 5 15 15m

1. Carport
2. Entrance Hall
3. Storage
4. Mechanical
5. Family Room
6. Bedroom
7. Cave
8. Terrace
9. Pool
10. Living Room
11. Dining Room
12. Patio
13. Gallery
14. Studio
15. Master Bedroom
16. Atelier
17. Green House
18. Kitchen
19. Service Bedroom
20. Service Living Room
21. Sauna
22. Fitting Room
23. Terrace
24. Ramps

This Page: *The main access to the house, showing the stone buttresses and the exposed cement "tray."*

Opposite Page: *Drawings and photographs show the careful adaptation of architecture to vegetation, to the extent of making the most important tree to pierce the house at its core.*

This Page: *The upper photograph shows a five-hundred-year-old tree (litre), which constitutes the only art piece decorating the room.*

Opposite Page: *The axonometric drawing clearly shows our stand as to extend architecture to the entire site.*

East Elevation

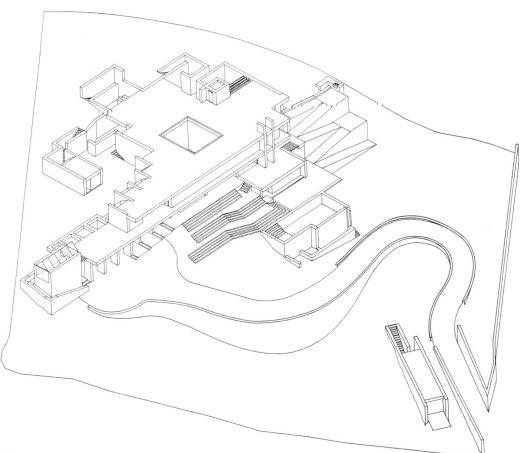

Axonometric View

La Cumbre House

Santiago, Chile

Christian De Groote Architects

This house is set in the highest portion of a neighborhood located at the feet of a chain of mountains towering over Santiago. The 10,800-square-foot (1,000-square-meter) site sharply inclines toward the street and is surrounded by magnificent native trees, giving shelter within its limits to a pair of very impressive specimens. The Manquehue hill stands directly behind the site.

The house was commissioned to us by a very young couple—of a rather unusual sensibility—with two children. They wanted an especially rich architecture, yet minimalist in finish; moreover, the spatial distribution needed to provide independence to different areas of the house without losing the unity of the whole or sacrificing the good relationship with the still-small children. In accord with the owners—and to make the house more sparing and straightforward—cement blocks and pre-fabricated slabs were used for the entire house. The materials were left exposed both in the interior and the exterior.

The project involved creating a large central space running the entire height of the building. Around this central space, the four different areas of the house were arranged in a spiral path, with a quarter-story difference between each. A staircase revolves inside the large central space, whose railing, based on a wall suspended in the air, both unites the spaces and grants them independence. The space of the staircase is crowned by a great skylight bathing all the rooms of the house in light. The double-height living room connects spatially with the dining room and study that constitutes the last level of the house.

Above: *The interplay of volumes and the consistent use of exposed concrete blocks as sole material, strongly contrast with the landscape in which the work is inserted.*

Opposite Page: *The floor plan's spiral development appears with great strength in the general interplay of volumes of the house, forming a dramatic contrast with its back of hills.*

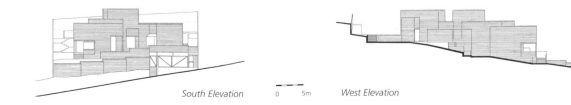

South Elevation   0   5m   *West Elevation*

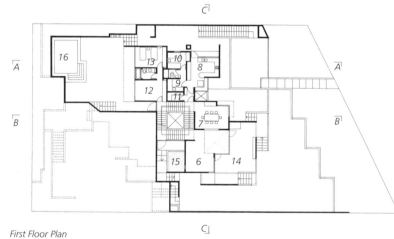

Second Floor Plan

First Floor Plan

Access Level

1.   Carport
2.   Entrance
3.   Entrance Hall
4.   Storage
5.   Mechanical
6.   Living Room
7.   Dining Room
8.   Kitchen
9.   Laundry
10. Service Bedroom
11. Pantry
12. Family Room
13. Bedroom
14. Terrace
15. Patio
16. Pool
17. Studio
18. Master Bedroom
19. Walk-in Closet

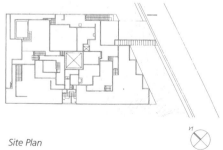

Site Plan

0   5m

This Page: *These photographs show the creation of intermediate spaces that enlarge the rooms, measure out the landscape, and create a continuous interplay of lights and shadows.*

Opposite Page: *The photographs illustrate how the architecture invades the site in its entirety.*

Section A-A

Section B-B

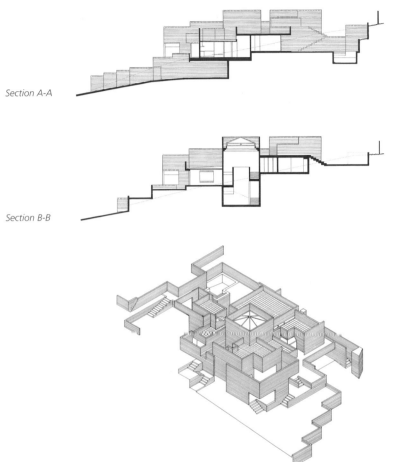

Axonometric View

Section C-C

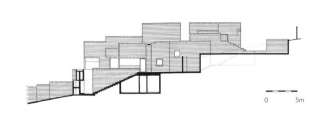

East Elevation

0   5m

This Page: *The axonometric drawing gives account of how the architecture rotates and expands itself, starting from the central hall covered with glass.*

Opposite Page: *The intermediate spaces, changes in level, and consistent use of concrete blocks give great unity and spatial richness to the house.*

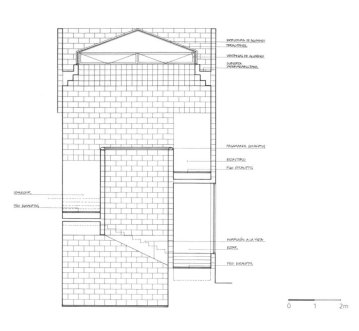

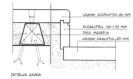

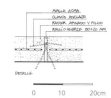

This and Opposite Page: Detail of the large central hall around which the different rooms revolve. This space dramatizes the displacements and grants different degrees of privacy to the areas it distributes. The height, light and generosity of this space bestow on the house a status exceeding its modest dimensions.

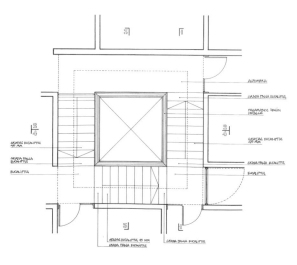

Main Staircase Section, Details and Plan

0   1   2m

Errazuriz House

Villarrica, Chile

Christian De Groote Architects

Located on the north bank of Lake Villarrica, 435 miles (700 kilometers) south of Santiago, this house lies on a property of about 247 acres (100 hectares), densely covered with native trees. From it there is a breathtaking view of the Villarrica volcano, located south of the lake. The site is relatively plain as far as the edge of the lake, where it falls sharply some fifty-nine feet (eighteen meters) down to the beach level and the water.

The challenge posed by this house was developing a project that architecturally links the upper plane of the property with the plane of the beach and the lake. The project also needed to safeguard the woods covering the site, the cliff, and the beach edge. A radical stance was taken, consisting of building the house on the stretch of ground between the cliff wall and the beach. Its upper terrace would be built at the woods level, without obstructing the view toward the lake and the volcano. The house itself becomes the element functionally and architecturally relating both planes.

The house, with its three stories and terraces, leans on huge buttresses of exposed concrete, and its capricious planimetry is a rigorous adaptation to the trees existing in the place. The house is entirely made of reinforced exposed concrete, both on the inside and the outside.

Above: The house, standing up facing the lake, is intricately immersed in the deep forest.

Opposite Page: In order to merge it with the landscape, the house was built behind the first row of trees. Again, the architecture stretches over the site and the beach up to the very lake edge.

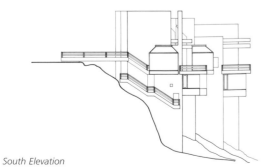

South Elevation

North Elevation

0   3m

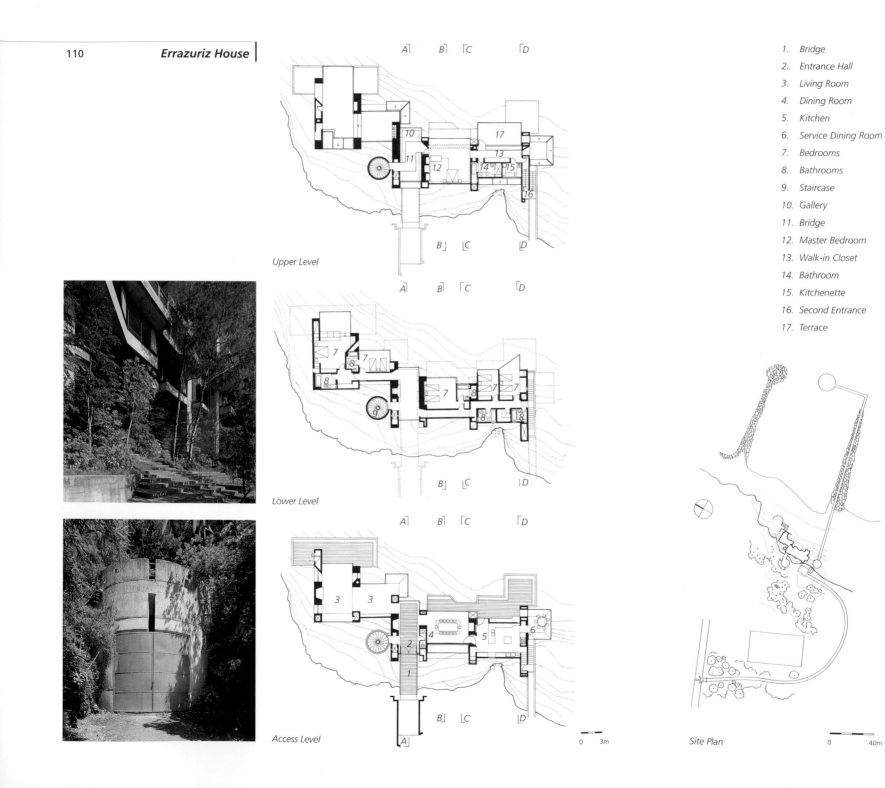

Upper Level

Lower Level

Access Level

1. Bridge
2. Entrance Hall
3. Living Room
4. Dining Room
5. Kitchen
6. Service Dining Room
7. Bedrooms
8. Bathrooms
9. Staircase
10. Gallery
11. Bridge
12. Master Bedroom
13. Walk-in Closet
14. Bathroom
15. Kitchenette
16. Second Entrance
17. Terrace

Site Plan

0   3m

0   40m

This Page: Upper photograph: the lake has a protected area for the anchoring of different sorts of pleasure boats delimited by two rocky breakwaters. Lower photographs: roofed area among the trees used as carport and as a rain-protected access to the house.

Opposite Page: Upper photograph: approach from the lake. Lower photograph: boathouse with upper lookout terrace.

This Page: *Beautiful concentric grooves embellish the modest concrete pavement of the circular access patio of this house.*

Opposite Page: *The circular access patio and the bridge leading to the front door.*

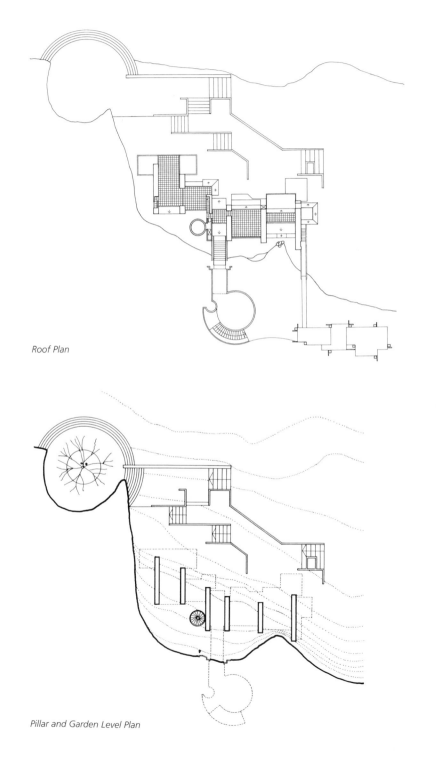

Roof Plan

Pillar and Garden Level Plan

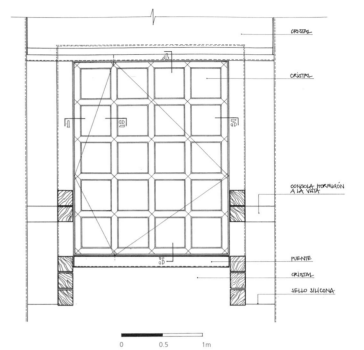

CRISTAL

CRISTAL

CONSOLA HORMIGÓN
A LA VISTA

PUENTE

CRISTAL

SELLO SILICONA

0   0.5   1m

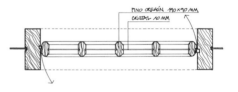

PINO OREGÓN 110×90 MM

CRISTAL 10 MM

This Page: *Detail of the access bridge and of the triple-height main hall, crossed by a wooden deck leading to the master bedroom.*

Opposite Page: *The triple-height main access hall, showing the treatment of the exposed concrete of one of the buttresses, which includes a small chimney.*

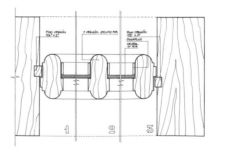

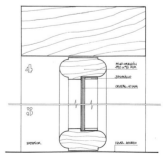

Main Access Door Section, Plan, and Details

0   10   20cm

This Page: *The spiral staircase connecting the different levels. Its steps are of solid oak, adze-worked in situ. The steps detach from the wall to allow the entrance of light from the upper skylight.*

Opposite Page: *The ceiling of the staircase forms a continuous helicoidal plane.*

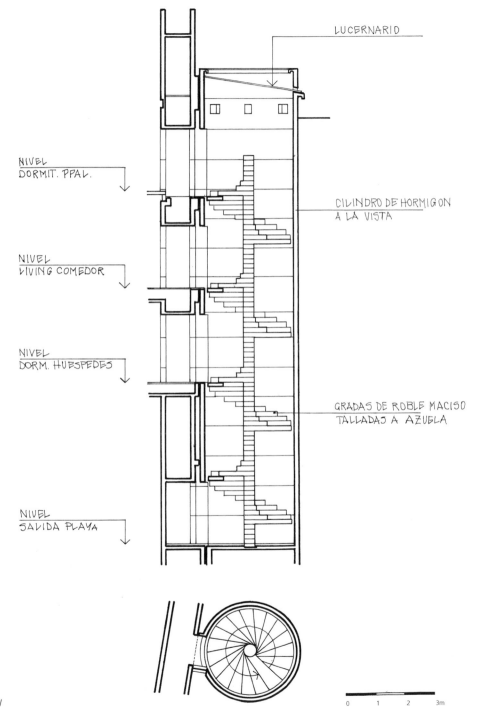

LUCERNARID

NIVEL
DORMIT. PPAL.

CILINDRO DE HORMIGON
A LA VISTA

NIVEL
LIVING COMEDOR

NIVEL
DORM. HUESPEDES

GRADAS DE ROBLE MACISO
TALLADAS A AZUELA

NIVEL
SALIDA PLAYA

0   1   2   3m

Helicoidal Stair Detail

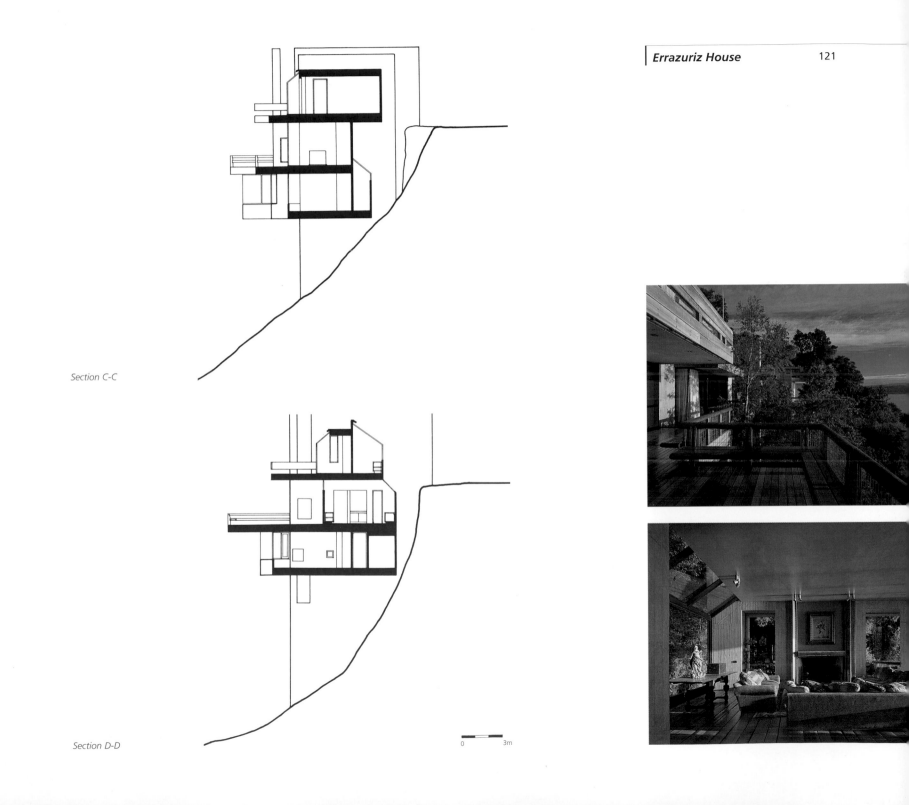

Section C-C

Section D-D

0   3m

The "El Condor" Group

Santiago, Chile

Christian De Groote Architects

To develop these three houses, a series of goals was established: to produce a strong group relationship; to create a geography adapted to the characteristics of the place and its vegetation—palm trees, conifers, thorny acacias, and poplars; and to concentrate on the relation of the houses to the large private park belonging to the former owners of the entire sector. The group relationship rests mainly on the incorporation of a cylinder as a recognizable common form and on a system of terraces stretching over the three sites that unifies the base of the cylinders.

The use of the terrace roof as a noble and fundamental feature of the house becomes particularly valuable in the Chilean climate and geography. The appearance of a "dual layer," a real architecture inside another, is formed by the cylinder that circumscribes an orthogonal architecture which sometimes approaches it, as others detach from or become incorporated with it, creating a series of intermediate spaces between the exterior and the interior.

The cylinder acts as a sort of "spatial hinge" that dominates the surrounding space, branching out in all directions. The role of this spatial hinge kept changing, from the first house built, the Fajnzylbers', until ending in the impressive volume of our own house, which makes the street look as if traced after its construction. The substance of the work, speaking of the three houses as a whole, was defined by giving a different treatment to each cylinder, leaning them on terraces with retaining walls of exposed concrete that grant them unity. Likewise, the stone of the cylinder of the Chadwick House is repeated in the retaining wall surrounding our house. Given the prevailing south and southwest exposure of the three sites, the cylinder also reflects the light coming from the north toward the interior of the houses. That is why in the El Condor House, the upper skylight plays the role of a window open to the sun in 360 degrees.

There is also a formal resonance with the upward limit imposed on the site by the El Condor street; still more important is the counterpoint of the cylinder with the inner orthogonal system and its capability to create such introverted and intimate spaces, to produce a surprising world of intermediate places between the exterior and the interior.

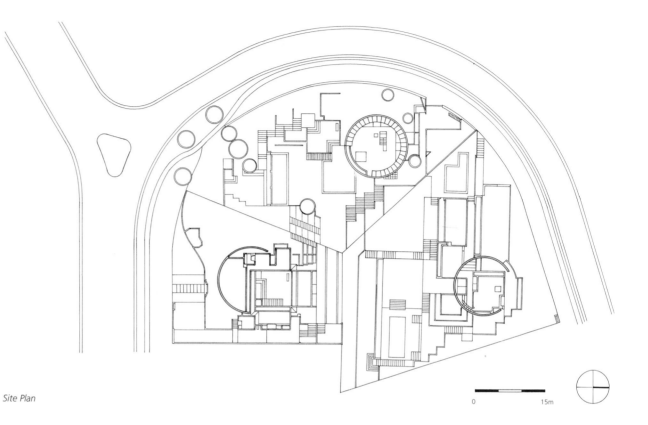

Site Plan

0   15m

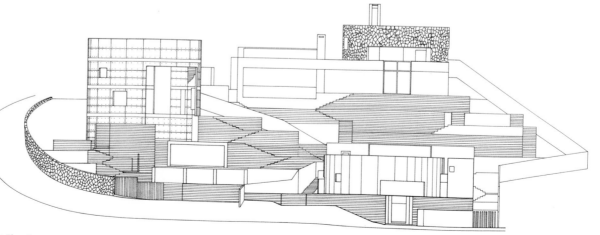

Group Elevation

In these houses—due to requirements of the first two clients themselves and coincidental with a search present in our last works—the need appeared not only to subordinate the window to the cylinders' planes, but to literally eliminate it. Thus, the three houses have several and very particular ways of relating with the outside. The interior of the houses is also stressed by their peculiar accesses: a tunnel in the Fajnzylber House, and a walled patio in the Chadwick House.

In the El Condor House, a succession of spatial situations consists of patios, stairs, turns, etc., which, on reaching the true access, have the visitor submerged in a world totally different to the outside one. In one of these turns, especially from the upper patio, the Rabat Park appears with a strength and richness not fully appreciated from outside. That is to say that in the three cases, and thanks to different resources, the outside world has disappeared before entering the houses.

This Spread: A continuous system of terraces and contention walls going through the three sites makes it possible to negotiate the great difference existing between the three cylinders.

Opposite Page: The three houses' ground plan and elevation account for the unitary treatment of the group, in which the three cylinders stand out for their height and materiality.

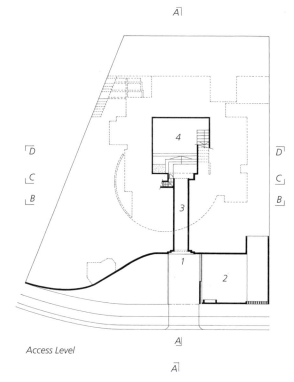

Access Level

Fajnzylber House

1.   Entrance
2.   Carport
3.   Tunnel
4.   Patio
5.   Entrance Hall
6.   Living Room
7.   Dining Room
8.   Kitchen
9.   Laundry
10. Service Bedroom
11. Studio
12. Master Bedroom
13. Walk-in Closet
14. Mechanical
15. Children's Bedroom
16. Upper Studio
17. Terrace

Main Floor Plan

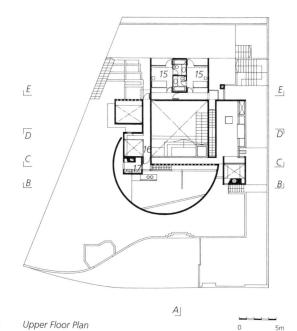

Upper Floor Plan

0   5m

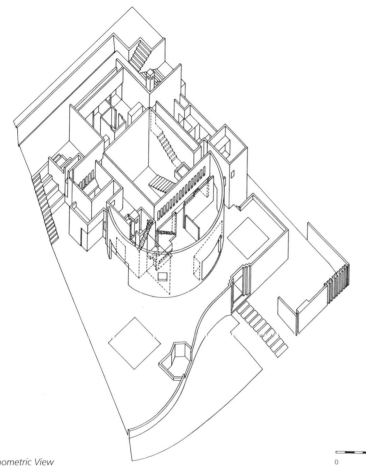

Axonometric View

0   4m

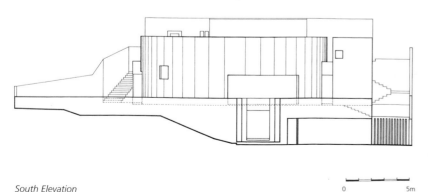

South Elevation

0   5m

This Page: *The Fajnzylber House, the most stern of the three, with walls of reinforced masonry, coarse stucco, and floors of polished concrete.*

Opposite Page: *The patio, an eight meter cube of polished concrete floor, is accessed through a tunnel.*

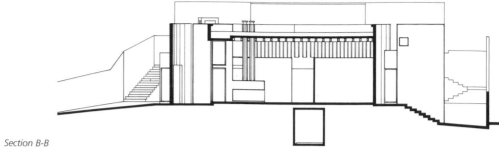

Section B-B

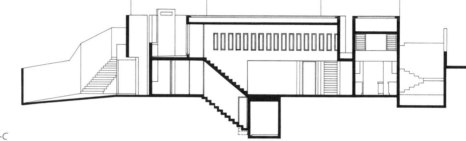

Section C-C

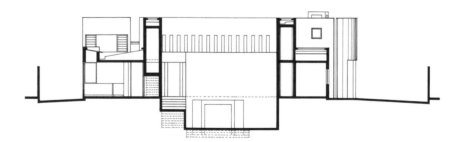

Section D-D

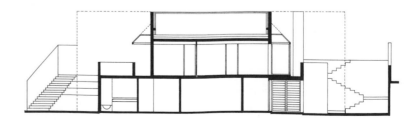

Section E-E

0   5m

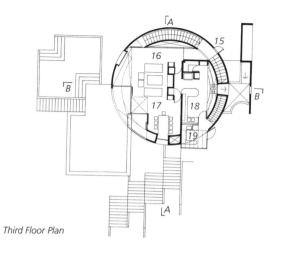

Third Floor Plan

El Condor House

1. Terrace
2. Studio
3. Powder Room
4. Library
5. Ramp
6. Patio
7. Main Entrance
8. Hall
9. Guest Bathroom
10. Bedroom
11. Bathroom
12. Service Room
13. Service Bathroom
14. Service Patio
15. Secondary Entrance
16. Living Room
17. Dining Room
18. Kitchen
19. Laundry
20. Master Bedroom
21. Master Bathroom
22. Roof Terrace

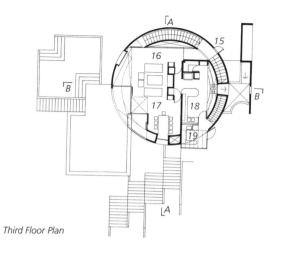

Second Floor Plan

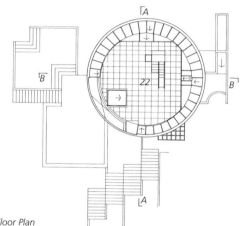

Roof Floor Plan

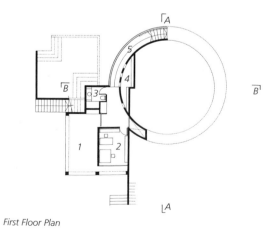

First Floor Plan

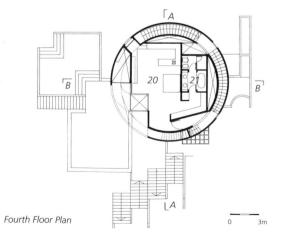

Fourth Floor Plan

0   3m

Previous Spread: The turret of the architect's house stands out as the dominant cylinder of the group.

This Page: The climbing plant in the upper photograph has been thought to act as a natural thermic protection against the cylinder's western exposure.

Opposite Page: The axonometric view shows the system of terraces and stairs thoroughly covering the site and acting as the turret's base.

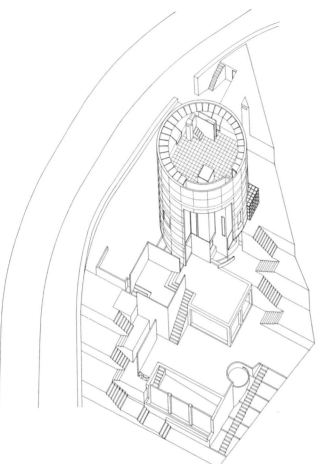

Axonometric View

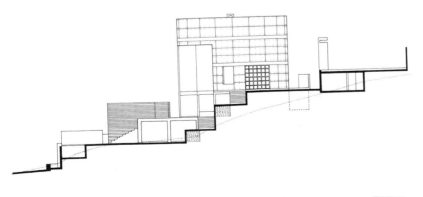

East Section/Elevation

0   4m

This Page: *The large circular boring of the inner cylinder visually enlarges the size of the access hall.*

Opposite Page: *The staircase detaches from the outer cylinder so as not to interrupt the continuity of the wall and to allow the natural lighting of the flight of stairs leading to the studio. The concrete molding is of plywood and it was given a single use.*

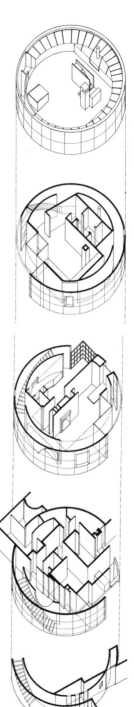

Exploded Axonometric View

0   5m

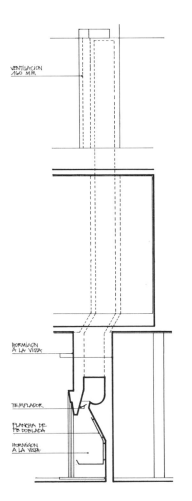

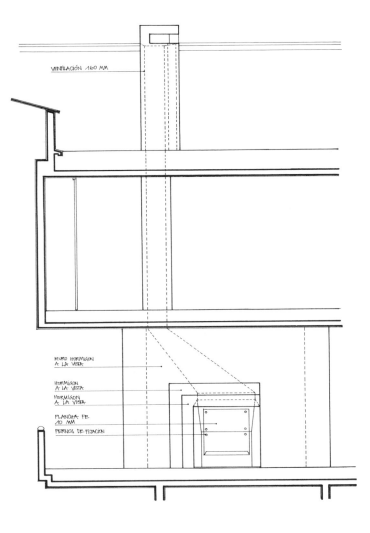

Fireplace Plan, Elevation, and Section

0   1m

Nevogilde House I

Oporto, Portugal

Eduardo Souto Moura Architects

In this rectangular plot, the boundaries were defined by party walls. A longitudinal wall crosses the building, separating the annex and service areas from the house itself. The structure is enclosed on the sides and open at the ends, with the bedrooms facing east and the living room opening onto a garden facing west. A square central courtyard organizes the circulation.

The house is designed to the limits of its site, and its equilibrium is precarious.

Were it not for the stone walls and the neighboring house, it would seem that nothing had yet been planned.

Above: *Addressing the contrasting nature of traditional and modern elements, an iron gate slides behind the stone wall, allowing entry to the garage and service areas.*

Opposite Page: *Designed for year-round use, this rectilinear house is masked from the street by a rough-hewn granite wall that echoes the horizontality of the residence. Traditional means of cutting and mounting the stones indicate strong references and respect for local typologies in this coastal town.*

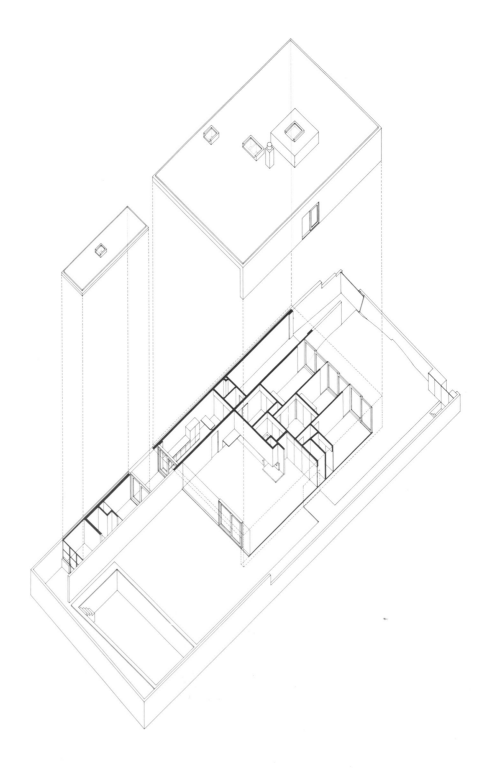

This Page: *Recessed to ensure protection from summer sunlight, the three bedrooms are defined by a curtain wall running parallel to the outer granite wall. The bedrooms overlook a small courtyard that is partitioned from the garage by an extension of a wall jutting out from the interior.*

Opposite Page: *After crossing a small iron gate similar to the one by the garage, a pathway leads to the main entrance of the house, located by a palm tree, and to the swimming pool at the end of the lot.*

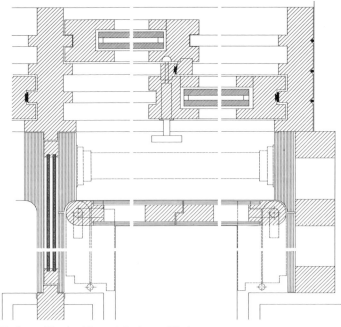

Horizontal Section Through Bedroom Window

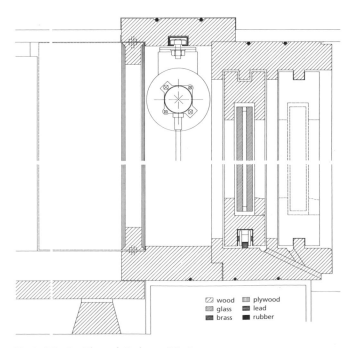

▨ wood	▥ plywood
▨ glass	▨ lead
■ brass	■ rubber

Vertical Section Through Bedroom Window

This Page: The bedrooms (top and center) are marked by the dissolution of interior and exterior boundaries. Windows form a seamless unit with ceiling, floor, and interior walls, and can be covered with movable screens for greater privacy.

Left and Opposite Page: A cubic and modular hall connects bed, bath, and storage areas. The mirrored panel and square skylight open the space and reflect their surrounding interior geometries.

Nevogilde House II

Oporto, Portugal
Eduardo Souto Moura Architects

T he site is made up of a set of separately acquired lots. Dislocating walls, moving the earth, choosing the stones— this was essentially the virtual making of the house. With a large and complex program, the house sits parallel to the existing site wall. The program is spread along a service gallery, the backbone of the building.

The various parts of the house can be identified from the south by openings that access the lawn. On the north side, only the door indicates the entrance.

From the street, there is only a gate, opening the place for us.

Above: Entry along a path reveals a series of granite columns rising in the distance atop a low-lying wall, recalling ancient structures. Recessed from view by a tennis court and surrounding flora and trees, the site appears to be an untouched extension of the landscape.

Opposite Page: The columns, in unison with the house and its surrounding vegetation, allude to ruins and anticipate the gridlike sequence of rooms and fenestration.

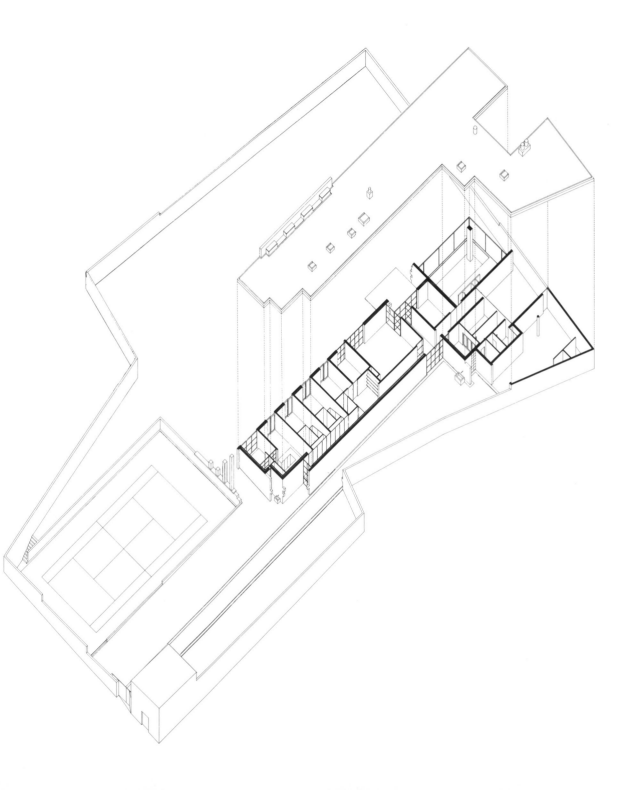

Left: *The main entrance is sheltered by a glass canopy.*

Opposite Page: *At the end of the patio, a large gate encloses an open garage. Granite fountains, situated along the property to collect rainwater, double as sculptural forms.*

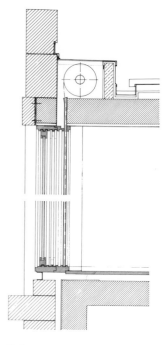

Master Bathroom

Bedroom

Indoor Swimming Pool

End of Corridor

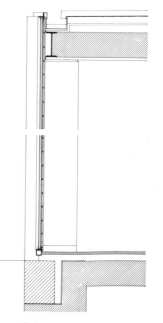

Entrance

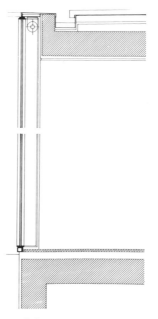

Kitchen

This Page: With marble sinks, walls, and flooring, the master bath is a study of reflected space. Stainless-steel-framed mirrored doors give access to the room and its shower compartment while expanding the interior. The indoor swimming pool is surrounded by curtain walls that eliminate spatial boundaries.

Opposite Page: In a finely articulated contrast of materials, a brass division connects the granite wall and wooden bedroom door. Corridors reveal the interaction of opaqued glass doors with brick and stone walls.

Alcanena House

Torres Novas, Portugal
Eduardo Souto Moura Architects

The initial sketches for the project resembled a nearby Roman villa. As the project developed, the house gradually lost that visual clue, with only the essential physical elements of the building remaining. The site had been marked with rows of vines—parallel lines cut by a nearly orthogonal system of paths. The house sits almost in the middle of a small hill, in the center of the site.

The house does not look like a single unit, but is spread out in three volumes—bedrooms, living rooms, and service quarters—around a central patio. A U-shaped gallery surrounding the patio links them together.

The project's reference axes (also orthogonal) do not impose themselves on the site's compositional lines. With their foci in the center of the patio, where they turn almost forty-five degrees, they enhance the landscape.

When the work had begun, an unnecessary water tower was demolished, a cellar was dug, and the steel window frames were replaced with natural-colored aluminum ones.

The surrounding landscape is reflected in mirrored glass windows amid white walls of stone and brick.

Above: *Viewed from afar, it is a site unseen, a white stone wall lying low against the hill and immersed in the surrounding topography.*

Opposite Page: *A road flanked by vineyards approaches the house, which is perched atop a gently rising hill. The residence, solitary in character, does not interrupt the continuity of the surrounding plain and sits in quiet harmony with the other, more distant houses of this small town.*

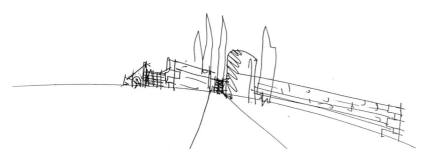

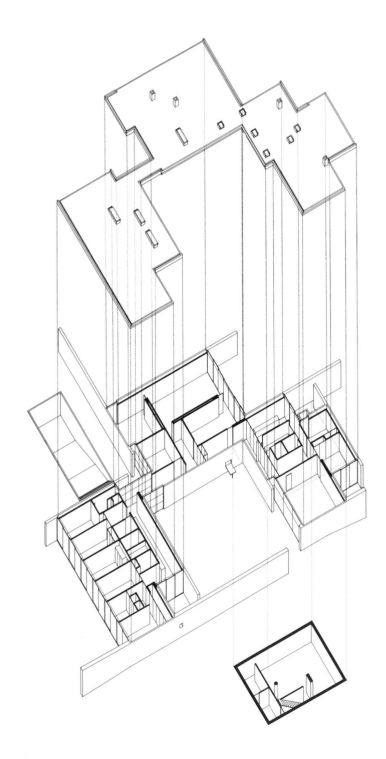

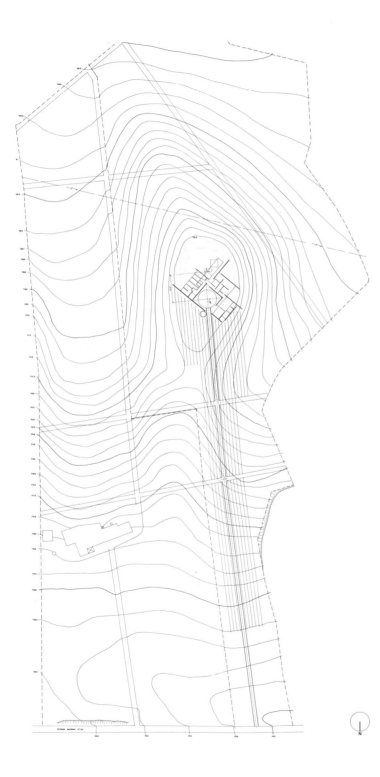

This Page: *Acting as a central unit, and sparsely populated with local trees and a rain catchment, the patio allows access to the main and service wings. The center photograph is of the patio facing the end of the corridor, behind the brick wall, where mirrored glass reflects and expands the space.*

Opposite Page: *The main road affords oblique entry to the central patio. Circular in shape and consisting of small stones, the patio is enclosed by a larger orthogonal frame. The garage is situated to the right of the entry.*

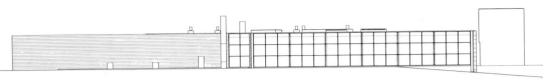

East Elevation

Section 4

Section 5

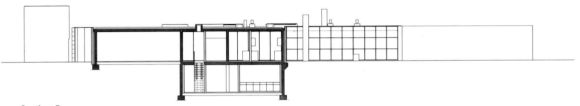

Section 6

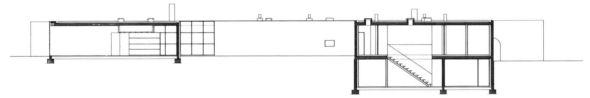

Section 7

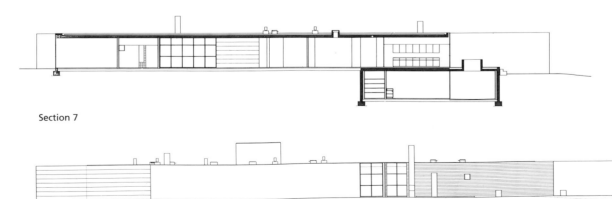

South Elevation

Miramar House

Vila Nova de Gaia, Portugal
Eduardo Souto Moura Architects

The site was essentially defined by a group of trees surrounded by granite walls. The granite walls were integrated, where appropriate, into the structure, forming several parts of the house itself—the garage, patios, rooms, and living areas.

A concrete slab above the ground floor serves as the roof and, when doubled over, closes the house at both ends.

On the sides, glass doorways allow one to see outside as far as possible: up to three meters to the road-side wall, between pine trees, and toward the sea that lies beyond the walls.

The project seems simple, and that is what was intended; as the Poet has taught, only "the exact word of any public use."
(Eugénio de Andrade, "Expresso," 5/23/87)

This Page: Trees and lawn act as interstitial space, mediating the dialogue of the plaster and stone walls that define the site.

Opposite Page: A granite wall, adjacent to a yellow volume and a white suspended ceiling, forms a private enclosure allowing entry to the residence.

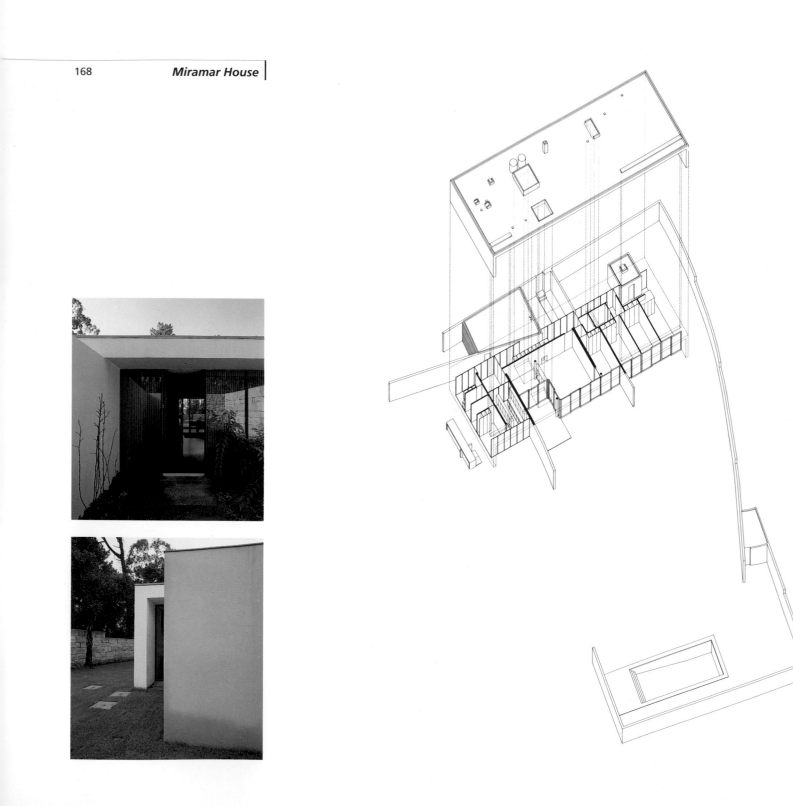

This Page: *Bedrooms, walled in glass, bring exterior views into private areas. The notions of interior and exterior space are further transposed in the living room. Timber floors, extended to the outdoor space, are enclosed by a cantilevered roof, glass panels, and a granite wall.*

Opposite Page: *The recessed entry patio affords views that cut through the house, revealing private and social rooms, and the garden just beyond. A rear detail shows concrete solids and glass voids interacting to provide volumetric definition.*

Right: *From the kitchen and service hall, and through the long and narrow corridor, access is given to the private areas—left side of photo-graph—and the dining and living spaces on the right.*

Opposite Page: *With doors closed, the entry area becomes more static in nature. When open, a fluid connection goes through social and private areas of the house. Mirrored glass doors expand the narrow space, capturing and reflecting the textures of the wood patterned windows.*

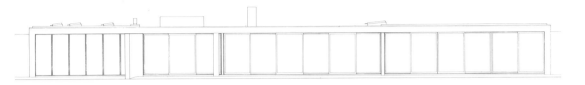

West Elevation

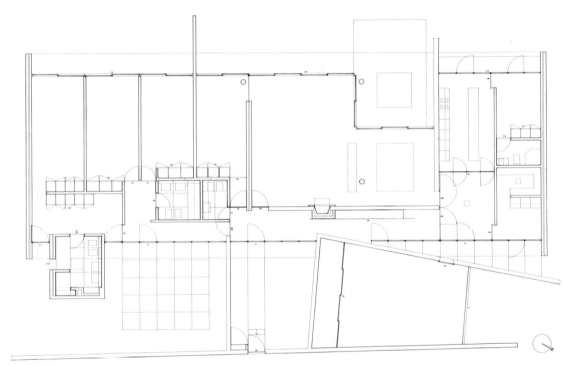

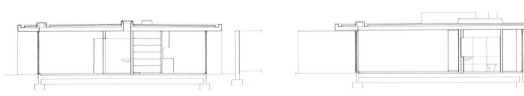

Section 1

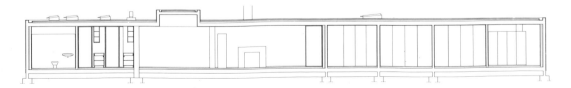

Section 10

Boavista Avenue House

Porto, Portugal

Eduardo Souto Moura Architects

This house is a collage of elements from other houses that I have designed, such as the Casa das Artes, and houses in Alcanena, Vilarinha, and Quinta do Lago. It was built using stones from a convent school and a ruin that was known as the "Sleeping Beauty."

The stones are fake in that they are not load-bearing. Leaning against concrete walls, they become the mineral texture of a painting. The fountain was once part of a window; the stones that make up the veranda and cornices, placed randomly, do not conform to standard masonry practices.

Incidentally, the "Sleeping Beauty" house was originally designed for Alves dos Reis, former director of the Bank of Portugal, who was arrested for forging banknotes.

Above: The curving path granting approach is encompassed by foliage that further conceals the residence from direct view.

Opposite Page: Modest in scale and spartan in character, the house barely rises above a low-lying granite wall. Much of the stonework is taken from stones from the site.

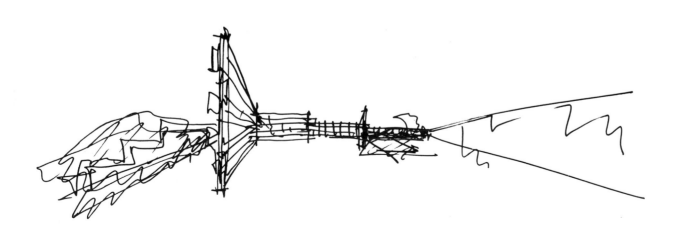

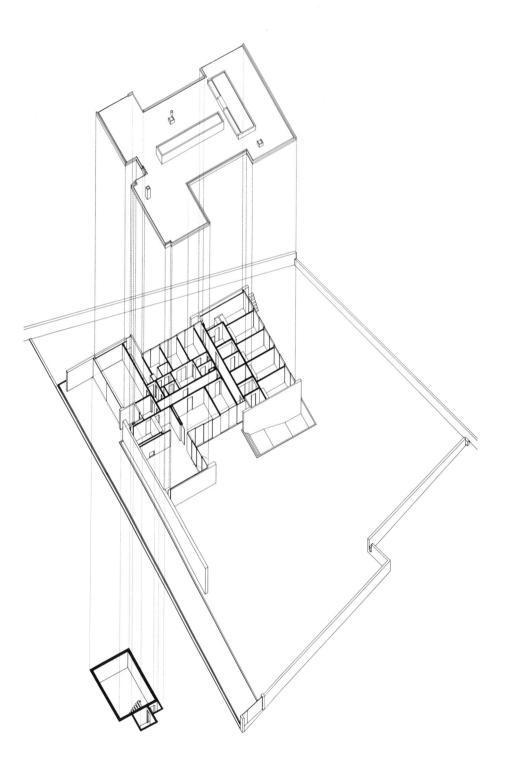

This Page: *From the exterior, living and dining rooms disappear behind intersecting mirrored glass panels. Seen from the interior, the ceiling appears suspended above the continuous, angular curtain wall. Containing shutters within, the windows are free to give multiplaned, panoramic views and unobstructed access to the outdoors.*

Opposite Page: *The outdoor swimming pool, lying next to the bedroom wall, appears as a reflective surface against the surrounding grass. The bedrooms are in linear procession and when their doors are opened, suspended ceilings are revealed.*

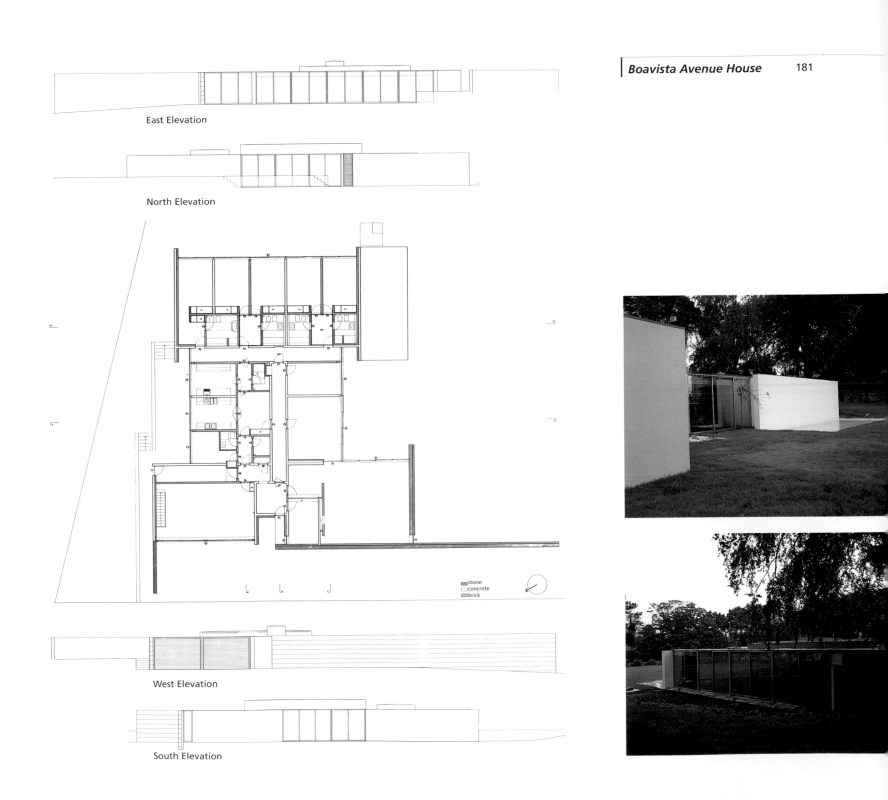

East Elevation

North Elevation

West Elevation

South Elevation

stone
concrete
brick

Bom Jesus House

Braga, Portugal
Eduardo Souto Moura Architects

One project consisting of two platforms, two stones, two programs, two construction systems, all forming two houses in one. The first level is for the children and consists of an "opus incertum," a stone box with doors and windows. The second level, for the parents, is a concrete box with a zinc roof and recessed floor-to-ceiling glass windows facing the balcony.

From the balcony, one sees the "market" and the appalling profile of Braga (the location of one of my first public projects, the municipal market).

Above: A water catchment takes on sculptural qualities, punctuating the terrain at the intersection of wall, path, and grass carpet.

Opposite Page: A rising, curved path gives way to this hilltop residence, whose contours and materials are reinforced by the granite wall comprising the first level of the two-story building.

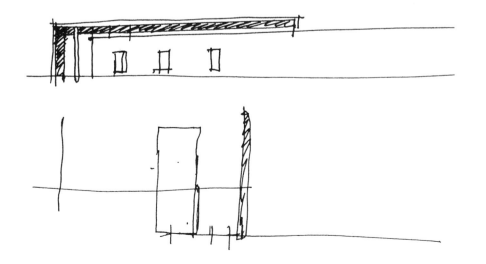

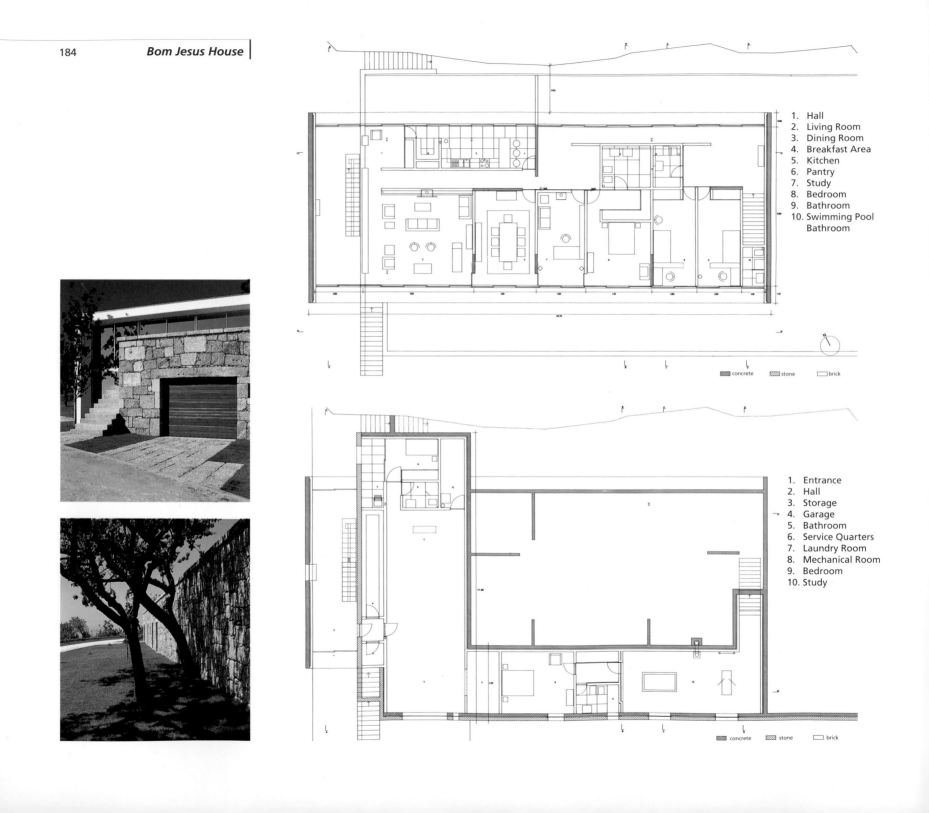

1. Hall
2. Living Room
3. Dining Room
4. Breakfast Area
5. Kitchen
6. Pantry
7. Study
8. Bedroom
9. Bathroom
10. Swimming Pool Bathroom

concrete   stone   brick

1. Entrance
2. Hall
3. Storage
4. Garage
5. Bathroom
6. Service Quarters
7. Laundry Room
8. Mechanical Room
9. Bedroom
10. Study

concrete   stone   brick

This Page: Geometrically harmonic, an open swimming pool flanks the southeast elevation. A detail of the entry facade reveals the stair's incline as framed by a white and glass cover. From the northwest, only the stair and wall, with a small, low, centrally placed window, are evident.

Opposite Page: The stone elevation, opening onto the garage, gives access to service and storage areas. Planes of the facade and upper tier of the house, though contrasting in material composition, are linked by their geometries.

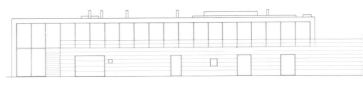

Southwest Elevation

Northwest Elevation

Northeast Elevation

Southeast Elevation

This Page: *Linear, wood-floored terraces, located at the front and back of the second floor, allow direct access to the outside through stone stairs.*

Opposite Page: *A curtain wall encloses a corridor along the northeast elevation, with bedrooms located behind. Adjacent to the swimming pool, it fronts onto a green, upwardly sloping terrain.*

This Page: *An interior stair connects the ground floor to the living room on the first floor. The iron railing and wood steps of the stair contrast with the solid volumes defined by the stone wall and terra-cotta floor.*

Opposite Page: *A linear skylight lets in shafts of light into the master bathroom. Some of the interior walls are mirrored to reflect the white plaster and grey marble used in the bathroom's construction.*

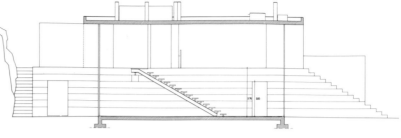

Section A

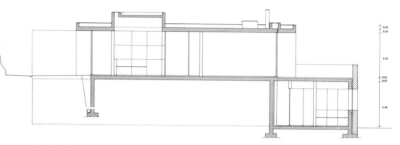

Section B

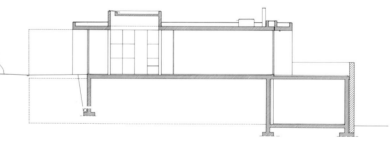

Section C

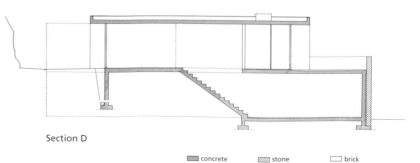

Section D

concrete   stone   brick

Baião House

Baião, Portugal

Eduardo Souto Moura Architects

The client required a weekend house with limited dimensions to be built at the site of a ruin. The basic project was to restore the ruin as a walled garden and to build the house to one side. Work began with the demolition of the retaining wall and preparatory excavation—producing the house in its inverted image. The house itself is a concrete box surrounded by earth, but open toward the Douro River. The program required a "Portuguese house," one that is integrated into the landscape, or, in this case, almost buried in it.

It was still possible, even with a tight budget, to include Technal window frames from France, Sika fabrics from Switzerland, Dow Roofmate from the United States, Belgian roof gutters and drains made by the Compagnie Royale Asturienne des Mines, Rocca bathroom appliances from Spain, Italian fixtures from Mamoli, and Italian lamps.

Local materials ranged from pieces taken from a demolition site in Barredo, tiles from Leiria, and cabinet-making from Paredes provided by Mr. Reis, with whom I had worked earlier in Miramar. This text reminds me of a local song entitled "I Want to See Portugal in the E.C."

Above: Ducts and vents in the roof push through the ceiling like the scattered stones that punctuate the grass above the site.

Opposite Page: With deep respect for the landscape, the residence was defined by an existing ruin and placed within its confines. A glass wall is the sole indication that the landscape has been altered in any way. The two coexist, the new structure blending seamlessly with the old.

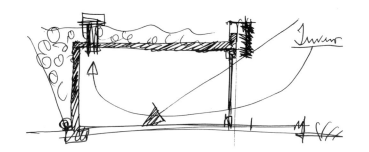

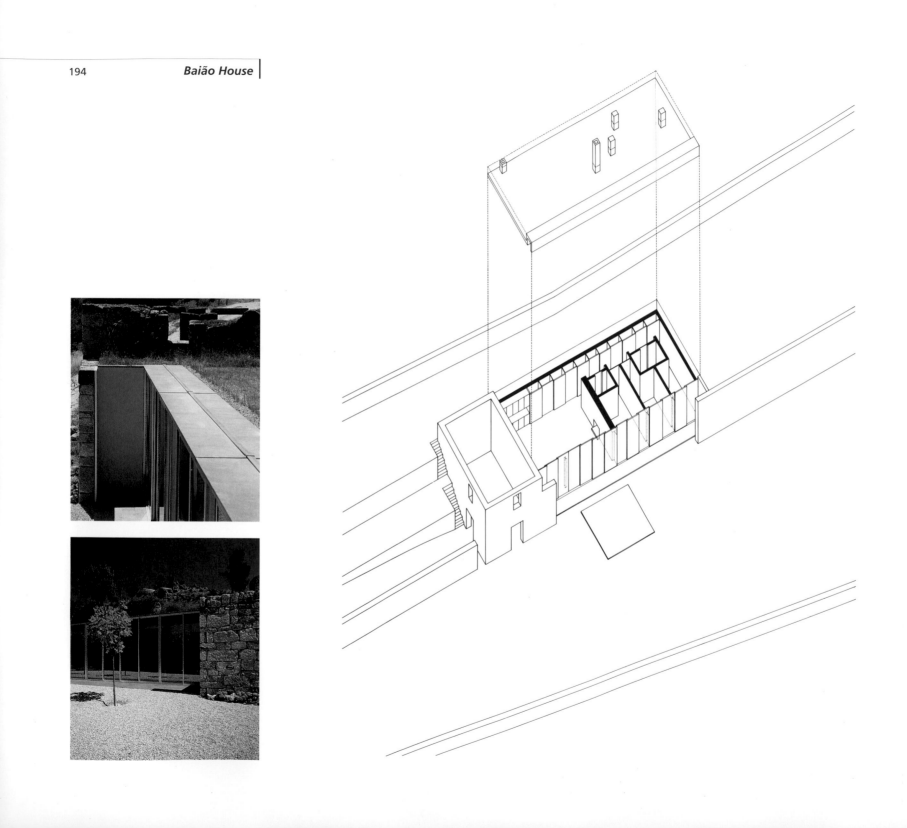

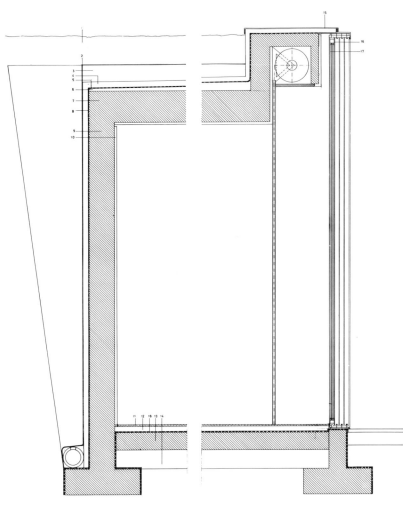

Section Through Front in Detail

1. Earth
2. Geotextile filter
3. Gravel
4. Thermal insulation
5. Steam barrier
6. Concrete
7. Lightened concrete
8. Steam barrier
9. Reinforced concrete
10. Plaster
11. Terra-cotta tiles
12. Concrete
13. Lightened concrete
14. Gravel
15. Galvanized protection board
16. Window frame
17. Double glazing
18. Waterproofing

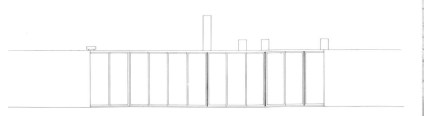

Main Elevation South 1/50

This Page: *Though condensed, a triple-rail system of windows allows the living space to be opened to the outdoors. Aluminum frames are inset between the wall and stone embankments.*

Opposite Page: *Wood-paneled storage areas, condensed along a single, narrow corridor, focus views to the outdoors. The warm colors of the wood contrast with the terra-cotta floors and the stone wall.*

Maia House

Maia, Portugal
Eduardo Souto Moura Architects

No excuses need be made for this house in Maia: despite the problems that come with every project, it turned out as I intended. There was no need to justify its form, typology, system of construction, or materials. This may seem strange but that's the way it was.

It so happens that for this project, I was both client and architect. A house should be designed by an architect for the architect. As an author assumes a pseudonym, an architect must assume an identity that adjusts to the client.

Only then can we respond to real needs such as shaving with the morning light, watching television with a fire burning in the fireplace, relaxing in the basement while the sun shines or the rain falls, or sleeping in the shade of a tree.

Analogical in program, orientation, and plot size, this house is based on the redesign of another house—the first one I ever built. The transmutation process was guided by ideas and discourse on inversion, collateral developments, and interconnections and omissions, in a path to muteness.

Architecture should be mute and opaque, but never deaf. This is probably the reason I was not asked to do the interior decoration.

Above: Windows facing the main road are veiled by trees that allow light while simultaneously keeping the bedrooms private.

Opposite Page: Compositional elements—walls, fenestration, and gate—are subtly linked to give character to the basic rectilinear volume. A textured palette is viewed from the entry, with metal, stone, painted stone, and plaster interacting.

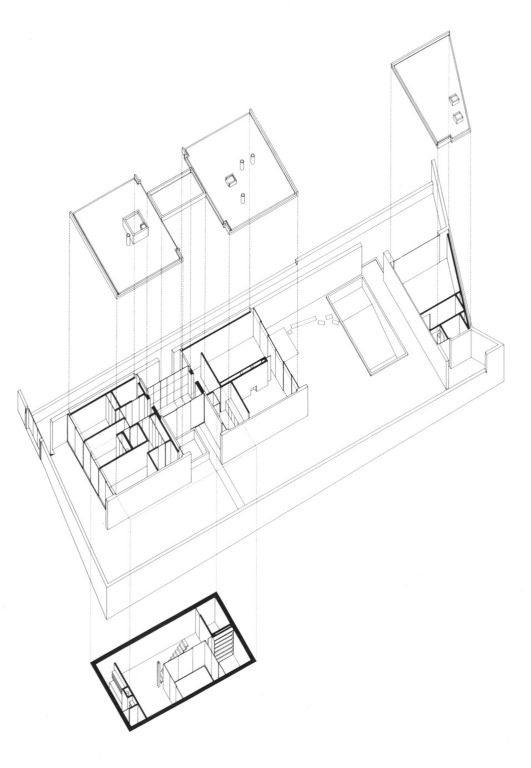

This Page: *A private drive, bordered on one side by a wall and surrounding fields, encloses access to the main entrance, patios, garage, and garden. These patios, with mirrored, wall apertures, are connected to a line of trees in the front, to an opening that lets light and air into the basement, and to an open-air dining area that leads to the pool.*

Opposite Page: *The plan divides the residence into two rectilinear volumes, which are enclosed by stone walls.*

Right: *Situated by the main entry, narrow rectilinear planes of diverse texture are centered around the attenuated volume of an evergreen tree.*

Opposite Page: *Details of the entry reveal the confluence of foliage, stone, stucco, and a glass wall with steel frame and wood-screen paneling. Opening confronting hall doors gives an overview of interior and exterior spaces.*

Basement Plan
(left)

1. Laundry Room
2. Pantry
3. Patio
4. Storage
5. Kitchen

Ground-Floor Plan
(right)

1. Lot Entrance
2. House Entrance
3. Patio
4. Hall
5. Bathroom
6. Bedroom
7. Kitchen
8. Dining Room
9. Living Room
10. Swimming Pool
11. Garage

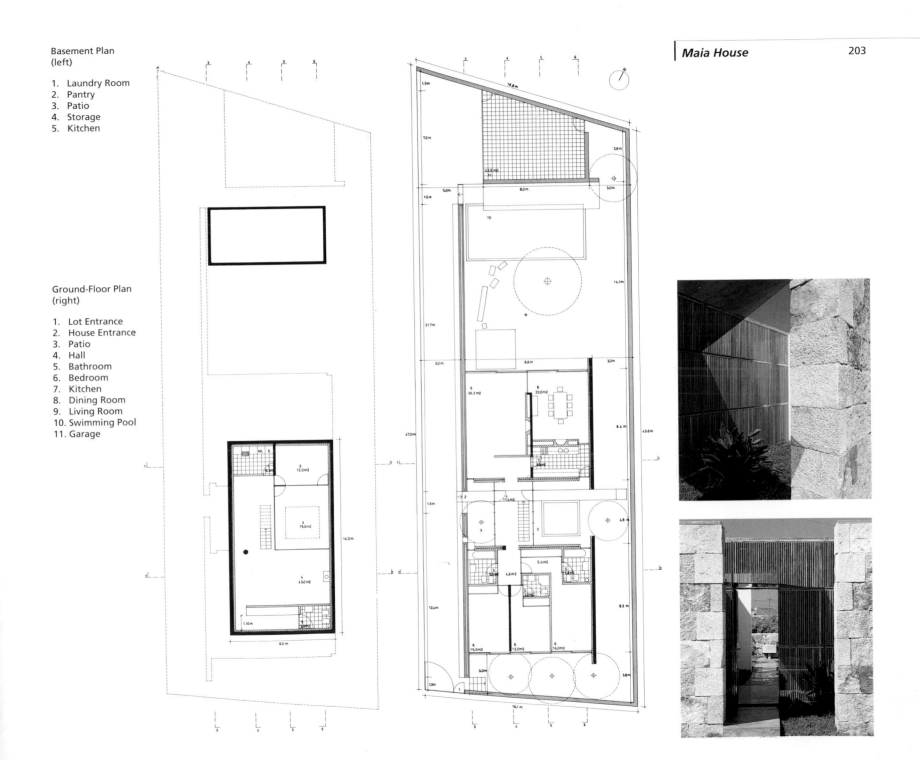

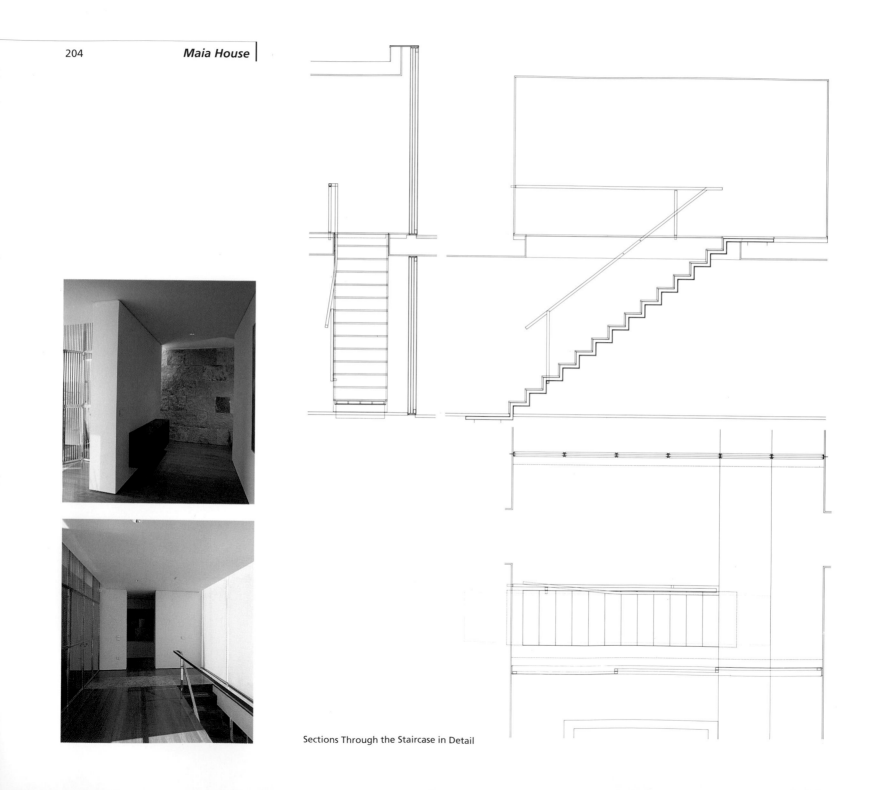

Sections Through the Staircase in Detail

This Page: *Composed of wood, the staircase echoes the surrounding floor pattern. Its stainless-steel railing reinforces the geometry of the window frames. A strip of marble visually connects opposite sides of the house.*

Opposite Page: *Interior views demarcate the tones, hues, and textures within the corridor leading to the living room. A staircase, located next to the second patio and facing the living room entry, leads to service and storage areas below.*

Tavira House

Algarve, Portugal

Eduardo Souto Moura Architects

P ortugal is a place of synergies, where one plus one equals one. The south is really quite different. This house in Quinta do Lago was designed in Macao, while thinking of Le Corbusier's Chandigarh. Looking at a picture on a calendar of the Church of Light in Tavira, I noticed that there were many analogies between Le Corbusier and the Church.

There are no coincidences in this house on the Formosa tidal flats. The view of the churches in Tavira was planned before work began.

Above: *Viewed from the rear, the east elevation rises out of the landscape, its facade punctuated by three openings.*

Opposite Page: *The stark form of an orthogonal tower framed by rectilinear volumes rises along the crest of a hill. Its pure geometries contrast with the encircling forest, appearing far removed from any surrounding contexts.*

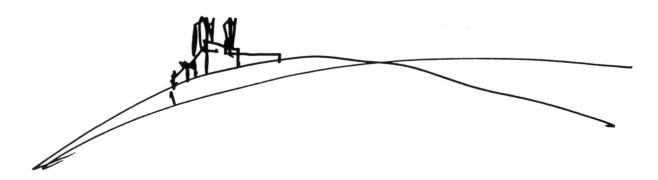

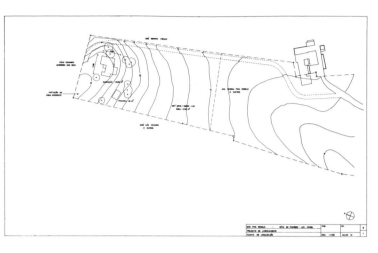

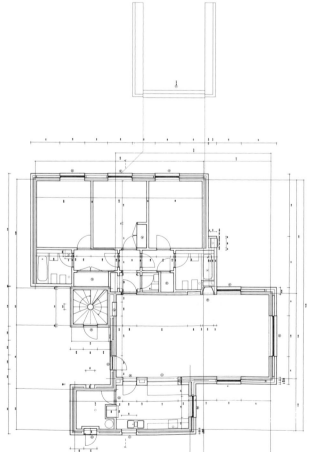

This Page: *The southern facade opens the living room adjacent to the tower. A staircase situated on the northern edge of the residence provides roof access, where geometric planes and volumes abound against visually contrasting natural panoramas.*

Opposite Page: *The east elevation overlooking the hillside contains three bedrooms. Heavy gridded wood shutters reinforce the monastic feeling established by the austere lines of the house.*

Right: Sliding shutters open to reveal symmetrically aligned voids that cut through the living room in modular repetition.

Opposite Page: From the inside, openings frame the changing landscape. Dialogues between inside and outside, light and dark, stillness and movement, are established by the original resolution of the apertures.

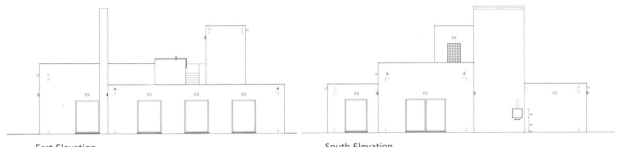

East Elevation

South Elevation

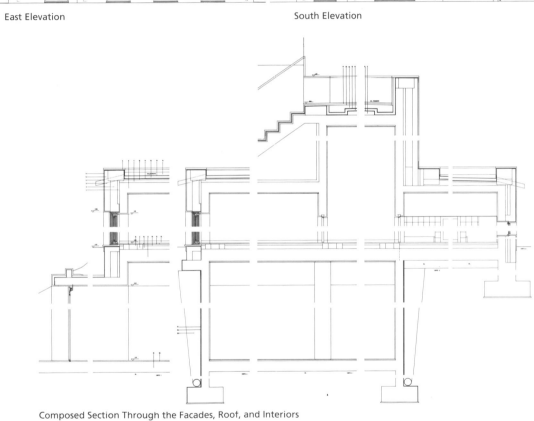

Composed Section Through the Facades, Roof, and Interiors

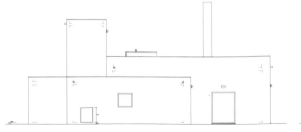

West Elevation

North Elevation

Mies House Pavilions and Second Addition

Weston, Connecticut

Peter L. Gluck and Partners Architects

Mies van der Rohe designed this private residence in 1955, based on his earlier model for workers' housing. He used window-wall units left over from the construction of his famous Lake Shore Drive Apartments in Chicago. One of only three Mies houses extant in the United States, the Connecticut house was bought in 1981 by a businessman who wanted to expand the very small house for use as a weekend retreat. Five years later, a new owner came back to the architect, requesting a permanent residence for his family. In the first phase, two separate pavilions were built, and in the second, the original Mies house was restored and enlarged.

The idea of "adding to Mies" was daunting. The challenge was to respect this icon of high modernism—by then a historical object—without mimicking the original. With respect to Mies and history, the design had to be contextual; with respect to the new owners, it had to function for their needs better than the original could. The task was to engage modernism as tradition and treat the International Style in a historicist mode.

Left intact as an icon, the original house became part of a composition of buildings, which included two separate but linked pavilions inspired by the plan of Mies' Barcelona Pavilion of 1929. One pavilion contains two guest rooms, a sauna, and a Japanese bath; the other, a large common room, complete with kitchen, for meetings and entertaining. The two are linked by a perforated steel screen that also marks the precinct of the outdoor pool.

The early modernist fascination with Japanese architecture provided another point of reference. Japanese elements are echoed in such details as the raised platform floors and the exterior walls that slide into glass pockets, leaving the rooms completely open to the outdoors. While the Japanese allusions are literal, the materials are high modern glass, steel, and aluminum. Mies, who used glass as a surrogate for walls, might have approved of their elimination altogether, a feat not yet technically available to him.

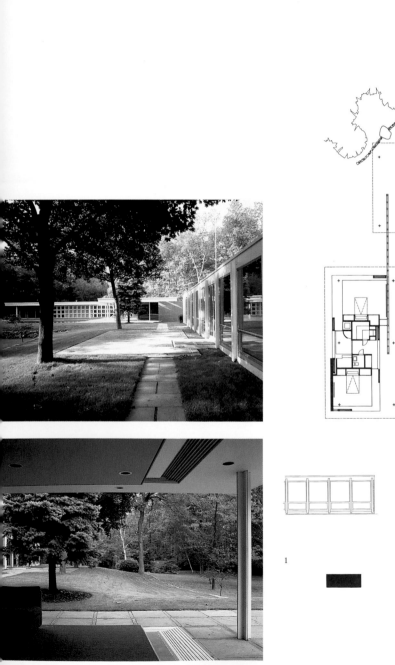

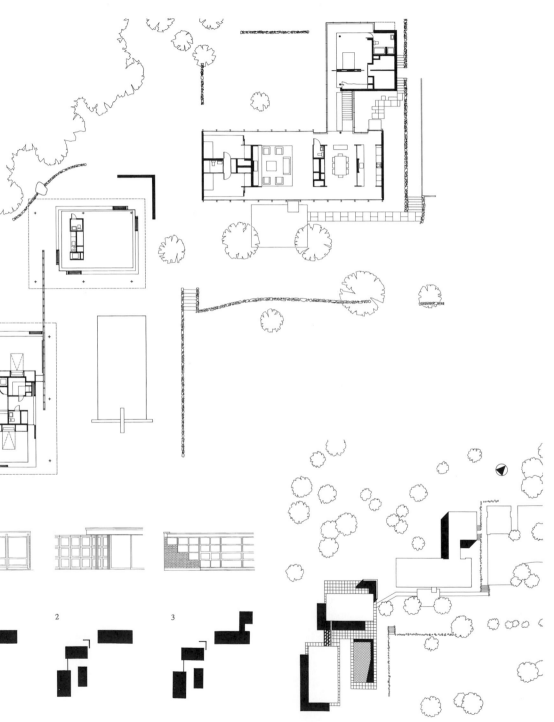

1

2

3

Above and Opposite Page: *Although intentionally set apart from the original house, the pavilions produce a composition that both alludes to Miesian theory and respects the integrity of the Mies house itself (right).*

Below Left: *The pavilions experiment with glass both moving and fixed: sliding glass walls open completely, and the perforated screen is glazed when enclosing a room, and open when out-of-doors.*

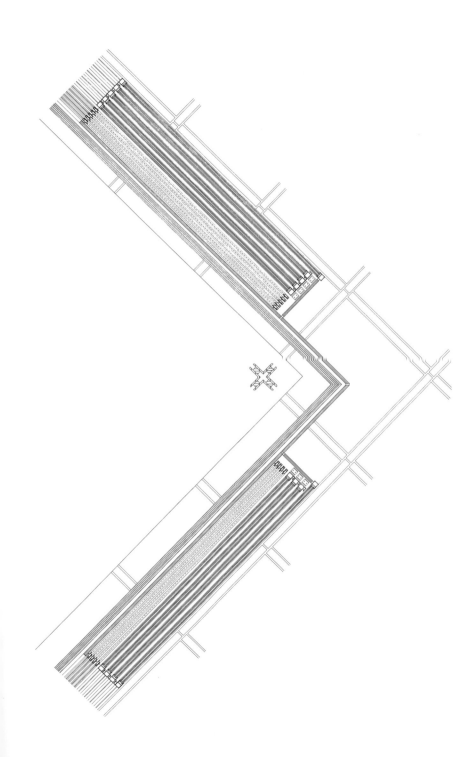

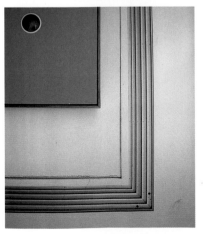

Left and Opposite Page: *The sliding glass panels and screens are stored in glass enclosures at opposite corners of the rooms. The dropped ceiling and raised floor demarcate the living spaces within the open pavilions. Reflections of vertical wall and horizontal roof planes on the glass panels create shifting patterns of opaque and transparent images.*

Above: *Accurate restoration of the living room included the replacement of deteriorated wood paneling, installation of the original travertine floor (designed but never laid), and repair of the steel roof system and window walls.*

Right: *The second addition contains a master bedroom, full kitchen, separate dining room, and basement playroom and utilities.*

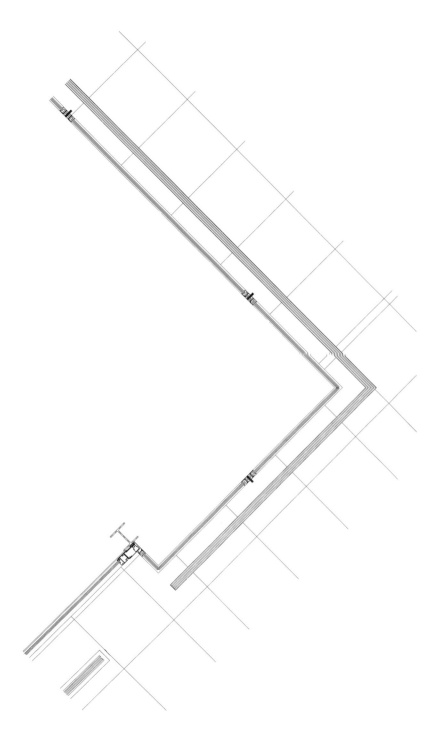

Above and Center Left: Extending Mies's use of glass, the design uses glass as an object itself, here shown at corridor to new bedroom and in new bathroom.

Left: A steel column (detail) supports a free-form maple desk in the study area of the master bedroom suite.

Farmhouse with Lap Pool and Sunken Garden

Worcester, New York

Peter L. Gluck and Partners Architects

Above: *The original farm buildings and the shapes of the new structure form a modernist composition that also evokes vernacular rural architecture.*

Opposite Page: *The sunken garden on the pool level—directly accessible from the gallery and master bedroom—is cut into the flat plane of the river valley site. Because the view is just below ground level, privacy is assured without the need for walls that would obstruct the open landscape.*

T his eighteenth-century white frame farmhouse, situated in an open field with a view of two silos and a hill-side beyond, presented a perfect picture of American rural vernacular architecture. The owners asked for an addition that would be twice as large as the original, and would include an art gallery and a lap pool.

The context demanded a design that would sustain multiple readings, allowing the original house to remain prominent in the composition without limiting the sculptural possibilities of the new structures. The new forms evoked the outbuild-ings traditionally added to the rear of farmhouses, and their shapes and materials linked them to the barns and silos on the site, all in an abstract way consistent with the principles of what the architect calls "contextual modernism." The same design principles developed earlier for the modern masters in the Mies and Wright projects, operate here with an anony-mous vernacular building, whose addition enhances the original both by respect and contrast.

Four separate forms contain the new living room, master bedroom suite, the gallery, and the pool, their separateness reducing what might otherwise be the overwhelming size of the new structure. To maintain an appropriate scale between the old and the new, the fifteen-foot high, ninety-five-foot long lap pool building is literally suppressed one level, so that the pool opens on to a sunken garden and terrace, which offers privacy without obstructing the landscape with fences or walls. The buildings both respond to the larger landscape and create landscapes of their own, which extend the house into exterior spaces defined by the combination of built and landscape form. Architecture does not stop at the outer wall of the building but integrally includes the space created by the reshaped earth and the surfaces composed by plantings.

The resulting composition now functions as a family homestead and retirement retreat, as well as a center for the display of local artists' work. The two functions are spatially and symbolically separated, but not remote from one another.

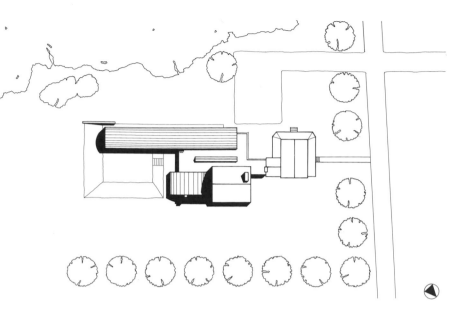

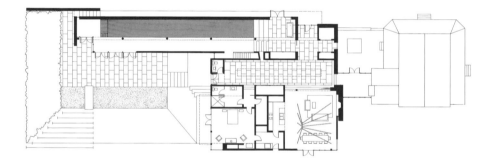

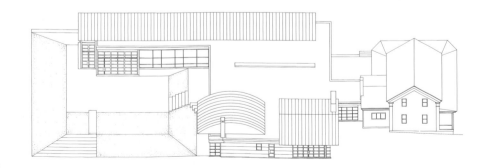

Left: *The additions to the Federal-style farmhouse are conceived as a composition of shapes that both contrast with and complement the eighteenth-century original. There is conscious ambiguity between the impression of multiple vernacular outbuildings and the reading of formal geometries.*

Opposite Page: *Color and texture of material enhance modernist shapes and forms. The pool area combines multicolor Indian slate, ochre stucco, aluminum-leaf ceiling, fieldstone wall, and polished natural-beechwood columns.*

Right: The structural wooden truss supporting the roof gives human scale to a very large space and implies differentiation within this multiuse room. Reflecting their exterior form, the master bedroom, bathroom, and the hall art gallery retain their formal identities.

Opposite Page: Conventionally inconsistent materials are used to express a contrast between formality and informality: the formal geometry on the one hand and the informal setting on the other.

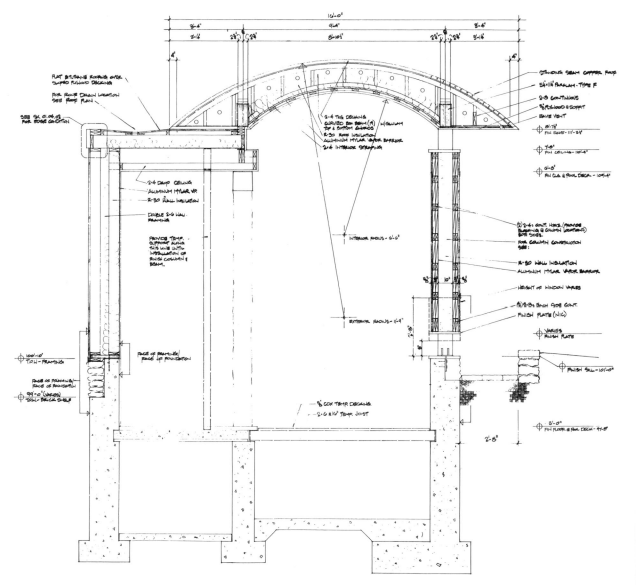

Bohan Kemp Residence

Buchanan Township, Michigan

Wheeler Kearns Architects

Sited just beyond the tree line where a stand of pines breaks and meadow begins, this house is approached on foot through rows of mature pines. A long platform—elevated upon pilotis to minimize the impact to the site both visually and environmentally—maximizes the experience of these two simultaneous landscapes.

Sharing roots with local Michiana polebarns, this economical structure of glue-laminated Douglas fir bents, braces, and decking stands on galvanized steel stirrups, keeping it clear of runoff and snow. Two small, concrete mechanical cores with baths above anchor the central space at both ends. Above the baths, small lofts overlook the central living space. Whole-house fans, coupled with transom windows, keep the tall volume well-ventilated during the summer. Protected under deep eaves of corrugated steel, generous decks and windows maximize connections to the two landscapes.

Above: Approaching the house through a stand of pine trees planted in a grid, the horizontal sweep of the floor and roof structure counters the verticality of the trees and forms a visual gateway to the meadow beyond.

Opposite Page: The structure and its elevated viewing platform sit gently on the sloping terrain. The building's visual transparency emphasizes the contrast between the warm interior palette and the subdued gray of the exterior.

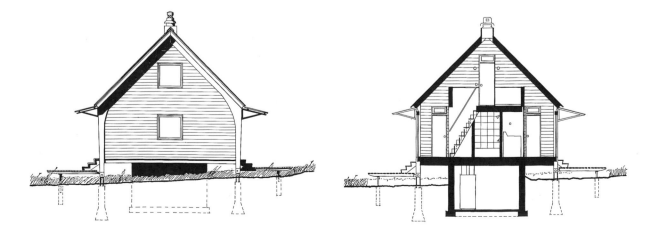

Bohan Kemp Residence

South Elevation

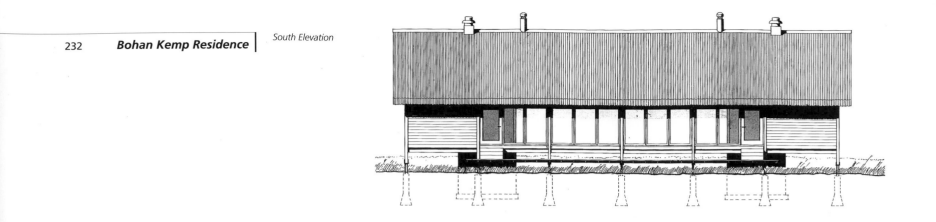

Floor Plan

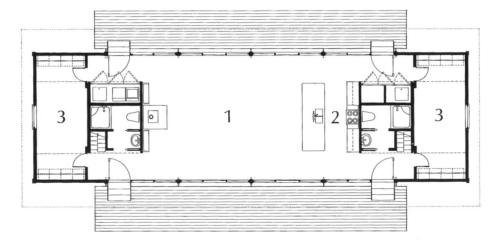

1. Living / Dining
2. Kitchen
3. Bedroom

Site Plan

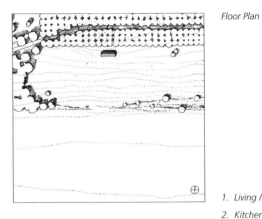

Longitudinal Section

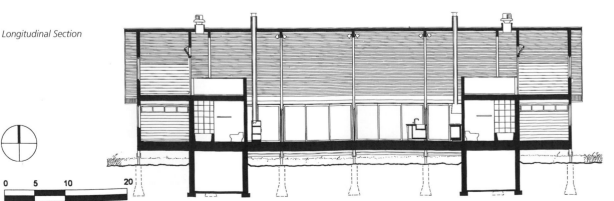

0 5 10 20

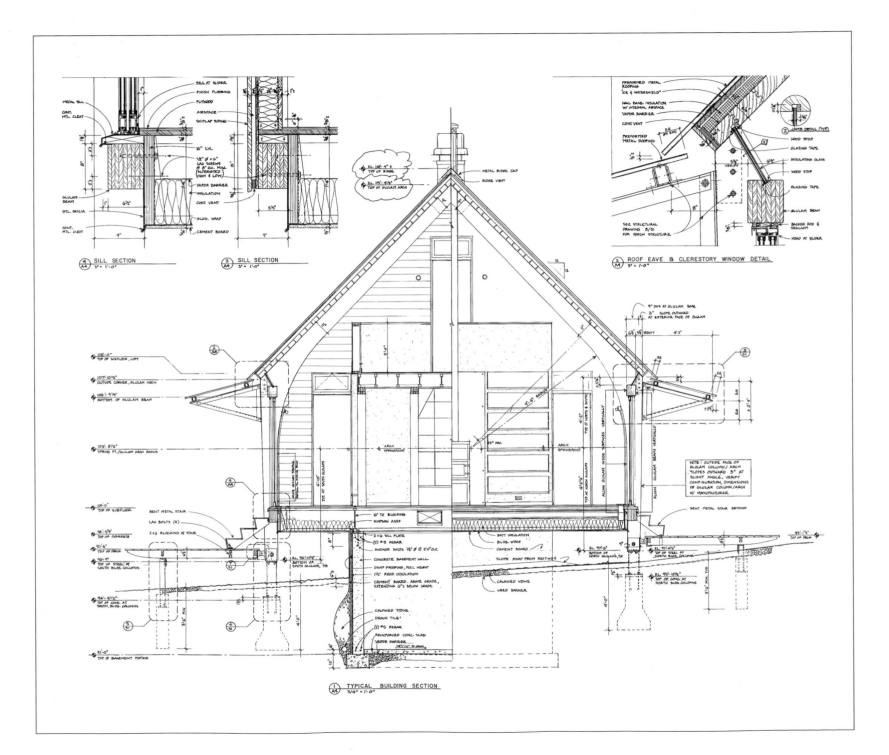

SILL AT SLIDER
FINISH FLOORING
PLYWOOD
AIRSPACE
SHIPLAP SIDING

METAL SILL
CONT.
MTL. CLEAT

16" LVL
1/2" Ø x 6"
LAG SCREWS
@ 8" O.C. MIN.
(ALTERNATED
HIGH & LOW)

VAPOR BARRIER
INSULATION
CONT. VENT

GLULAM
BEAM

MTL. FASCIA
CONT.
MTL. CLEAT

BLDG. WRAP
CEMENT BOARD

④ SILL SECTION
A4 3" = 1'-0"

③ SILL SECTION
A4 3" = 1'-0"

PREFORMED METAL
ROOFING
"ICE & WATERSHIELD"

NAIL BASE INSULATION
W/ INTEGRAL AIRSPACE
VAPOR BARRIER

CONT. VENT

PREFORMED
METAL ROOFING

② JAMB DETAIL (TYP.)

HOOD STOP
GLAZING TAPE
INSULATING GLASS
WOOD STOP
GLAZING TAPE
GLULAM BEAM
BACKER ROD &
SEALANT
HEAD AT SLIDER

SEE STRUCTURAL
DRAWING S/51
FOR PORCH STRUCTURE

② ROOF EAVE & CLERESTORY WINDOW DETAIL
A4 3" = 1'-0"

EL. 108'-5" ±
TOP OF RIDGE

EL. 113'-4½"
TOP OF GLULAM ARCH

METAL RIDGE CAP
RIDGE VENT

9" DIA AT GLULAM BASE
3" SLOPE OUTWARD
AT EXTERIOR FACE OF GLULAM

108'-0"
TOP OF SUBFLOOR, LOFT

107'-10½"
OUTSIDE CORNER, GLULAM ARCH

106'-9¼"
BOTTOM OF GLULAM BEAM

ARCH
SPRINGPOINT

ARCH
SPRINGPOINT

103'-8½"
SPRING PT./GLULAM ARCH RADIUS

NOTE: OUTSIDE FACE OF
GLULAM COLUMN/ARCH
"SLOPES OUTWARD 3" AT
SLIGHT ANGLE. VERIFY
CONFIGURATIONS, DIMENSIONS
OF GLULAM COLUMN/ARCH
W/ MANUFACTURER

100'-0"
TOP OF SUBFLOOR

BENT METAL STAIR
LAG BOLTS (4)
2 x 6 BLOCKING AT STAIR

98'-5¾"
TOP OF CONC GTB

97'-6"
TOP OF DECK

96'-9"
TOP OF STEEL AT
SOUTH BLDG. COLUMNS

16" TJI BLOCKING
SIMPSON A35F

2 x 6 SILL PLATE
(2) #5 REBAR
ANCHOR BOLTS ½" Ø @ 2'-0" O.C.

CONCRETE BASEMENT WALL

DAMP PROOFING, FULL HEIGHT
1½" RIGID INSULATION
CEMENT BOARD. ABOVE GRADE,
EXTENDING 6"± BELOW GRADE

BENT METAL STAIR BEYOND

BATT INSULATION
BLDG. WRAP
CEMENT BOARD

SLOPE AWAY FROM FOOTINGS

CRUSHED STONE
WEED BARRIER

EL. 97'-6"
BOTTOM OF
NORTH GLULAMS, TYP.

EL. 97'-6"
TOP OF STEEL AT
NORTH BLDG. COLUMNS

TOP OF DECK

95'-10"
BOTTOM OF
SOUTH GLULAMS, TYP.

94'-5½"
TOP OF CONC AT
SOUTH BLDG. COLUMNS

CRUSHED STONE
DRAIN TILE
(2) #5 REBAR
REINFORCED CONC. SLAB
VAPOR BARRIER

EL. 95'-10½"
TOP OF CONC AT
NORTH BLDG. COLUMNS

91'-0"
TOP OF BASEMENT FOOTING

① TYPICAL BUILDING SECTION
A4 3/4" = 1'-0"

LaPoint Residence

Buchanan Township, Michigan

Wheeler Kearns Architects

Before construction on this elevated wooded plateau in southwestern Michigan, the owners of this house approached Wheeler Kearns Architects with a modest budget, expressing a desire: a retreat-like atmosphere with simple modern spaces. The program is concise; bedrooms below and an open living space lifted above. Because the owners could not afford a separate screened porch, the communal space essentially became one, with views in all directions. In the winter, the surrounding trees shed their leaves and reveal a cornfield to the north and a lake to the south visible through a thicket of tree trunks.

Means of construction were kept very simple. A two-story, rigid moment-frame rests on a shallow "slab on grade" foundation. The upper floor utilizes plywood web joists fifty-two feet (sixteen meters) long, which run the long direction of the house. The joists provide greater efficiencies of construction as well as the stiffness of continuous spans over interior supporting walls. Top chord hung trusses support the roof while providing an internal lighting cove. The continuous envelope of off-the-shelf sliding glass doors on the second floor establishes a disciplined module for the overall dimensions. The only interruptions of the view are created by structural steel shear walls that form the backdrop for freestanding fireplaces at both ends. The changing seasons, light, and landscape become part of the architectural experience in a house separated from—yet integrated with—its surroundings, fulfilling the client's desire to live amongst the trees.

Above: The house seen from the road below to the southwest.

Opposite Page: The ground-floor bedrooms receive light and ventilation from the sides, reducing the entry elevation to an elemental expression of access with elevated living space.

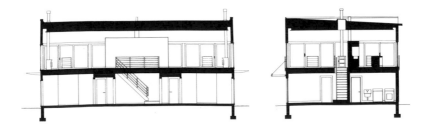

South Elevation

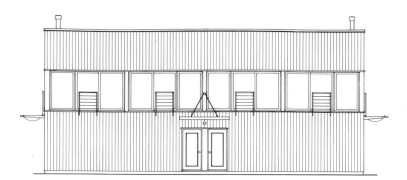

Second Floor Plan

1. Entry
2. Bedroom
3. Utility
4. Living / Dining
5. Kitchen

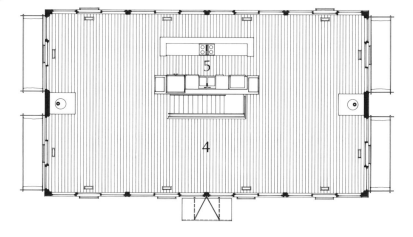

Site Plan

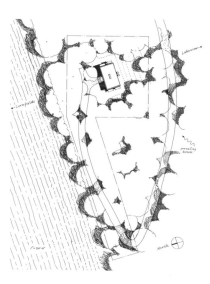

First Floor Plan

0   5   10   20

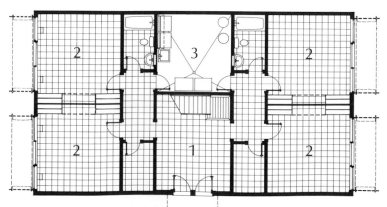

Opposite Page: *To keep costs within budget, the modules of the structural bay and the sliding glass doors are coordinated for maximum efficiency and strictly maintained.*

Left: *The primary structure uses built-up microlam columns and beams, with embedded steel plates at the joints to form a structurally rigid moment-frame. Second floor structure runs fifty-two feet (sixteen meters) in the long direction. Roof trusses span the opposite short direction for structural efficiency.*

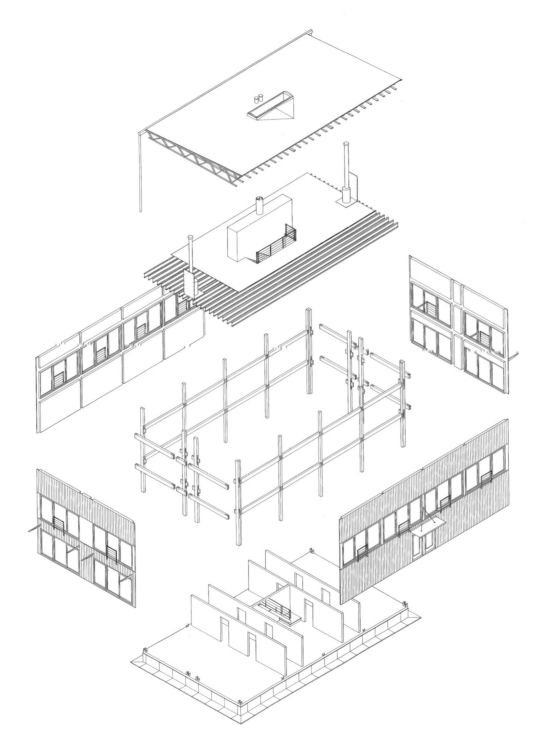

Above: *Entry hall stair to the upper living spaces. Tiled in a cool slate, the first level features a pad of wood dropping down into the foyer as an offering of the warmth above.*

Opposite Page: *One ascends the stair alongside a blue mass, which terminates short of the celling. At the top of the stair the expansive view of trees all around reveals itself. The physical warmth provided by wood stoves at either end of the space echoes the warm color of the southern yellow pine flooring.*

Mussman Residence

Ogden Dunes, Indiana

Wheeler Kearns Architects

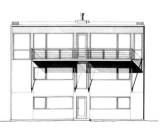

Having secured a vacant lot on a bluff behind an existing Lake Michigan beach house, a young family initially sought to build a sprawling one-story house. It had to accommodate the parents, their two young children, and a grandmother confined to a wheelchair. Budget constraints required exceptional economy in construction.

To simultaneously take advantage of a cost effective, compact volume and also maximize extraordinary views envisioned from a higher elevation, the architects developed a three-story scheme that utilized an unconventional arrangement of spaces around a central spine of circulation. Elevated to the third floor, the main living spaces achieve an uninterrupted view of Lake Michigan over the neighboring beach house. The second floor comprises the master suite and two children's bedrooms. The ground floor accommodates the grandmother's apartment and a family room.

To preserve compactness, a three-foot- (one-meter-) wide zone through the center of the house combines the stair, hallway, and lightwell. It contains a straight run stair designed to gradually reveal a view of the lake as one ascends from the entry. The middle landing of the stair serves as a hall with entries to the master suite and bedrooms. Aligned with the stair and matching its width is an overhead skylight that filters daylight through a third-floor aluminum grate and through the open grate stair treads to the ground floor hall below.

Above: The house sits on a high plateau of ground, with limited site access.

Below and Opposite Page: The blue-painted walls of the central stair are load-bearing. Stair treads span from wall to wall, with no stringers required. From the entry court elevation, vertical blue mullions suggest the structural system within.

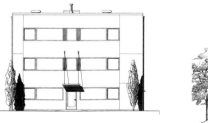

Mussman Residence

1. Entry

2. Recreation

3. In-Law Living

4. In-Law Bedroom

5. Bedroom

6. Sitting

7. Living

8. Dining

9. Kitchen

Third Floor Plan

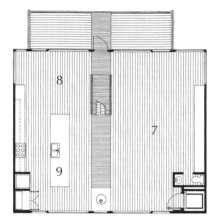

Second Floor Plan

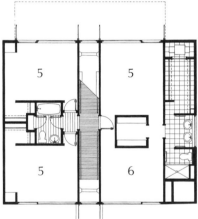

First Floor Plan

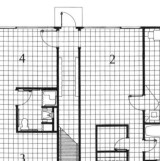

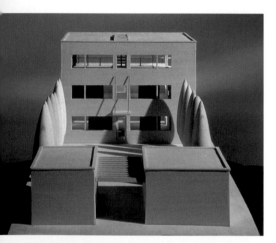

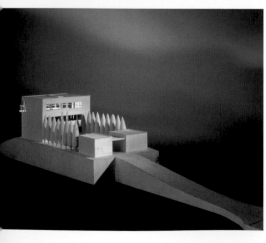

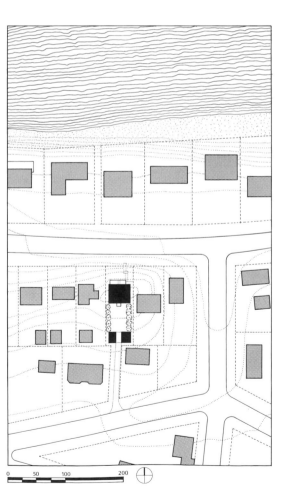

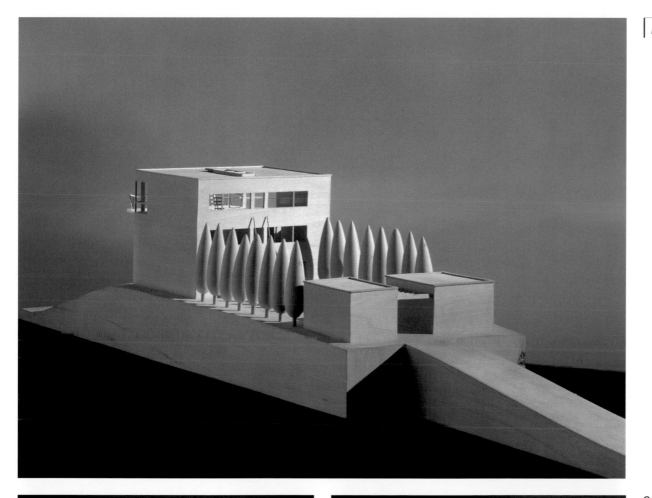

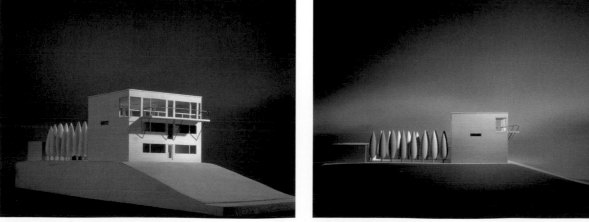

Opposite Page: *The model and site drawings include future garages and a trellis designed to complete the approach sequence to the house.*

Left: *The house sits on the edge of the plateau, with the ground quickly sloping away toward Lake Michigan.*

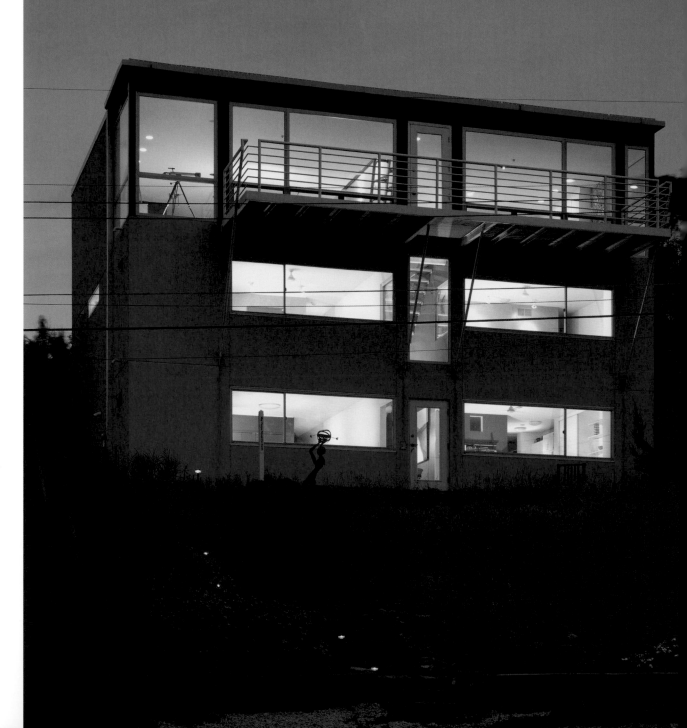

Right: *The lake elevation of the house reveals the expanded breadth of glass and upper deck. Detached from the main volume, the steel-framed wood deck appears a separate entity.*

Opposite Page: *The house sits high above surrounding residences and the street to take the best advantage of lake views. An exploded axonometric drawing illustrates the simplicity of construction.*

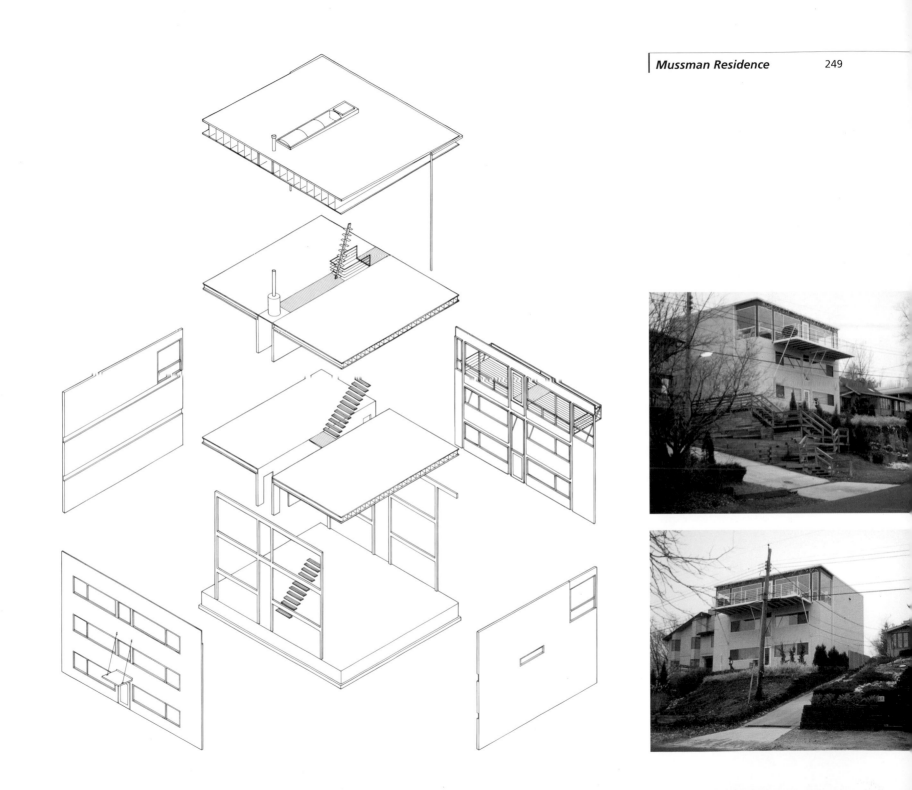

Essex Residence and Office

Chicago, Illinois

Wheeler Kearns Architects

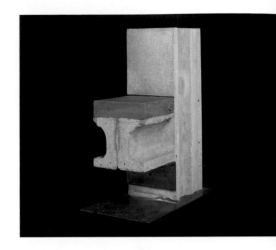

Wheeler Kearns Architects searched with a husband-and-wife graphic design team for an existing building to house their small office and their growing family. Nothing was found within their means, so they looked for land and selected a vacant lot forty-eight feet (fifteen meters) wide on a busy commercial street in the Wicker Park neighborhood. It contained twelve feet (four meters) of buried subsoil debris and zoning required a fire-resistant structure. The scope and program were set within a budget of two-thirds of what one typically could afford.

The architects quickly deemed conventional solutions untenable; with the scope fixed and the understanding that roughly half the cost of construction is material and the other half labor, the only remaining solution was to limit labor on site, hence prefabrication. An exploration of alternatives yielded an industrial pre-cast concrete system typically utilized for warehouses and factories.

__Opposite Page and Left:__ A simple, taut volume capitalizes on the reductive attitude and minimalist aesthetic employed. Insulated-core concrete wall panels isolate the spaces within the building from the noise of its surrounding urban neighborhood. Windows and doors are placed in cadence with these load-bearing panels and integrate with their structural logic.

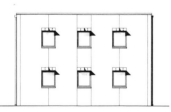

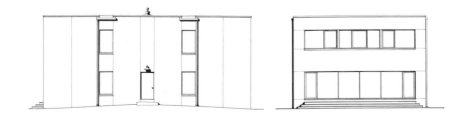

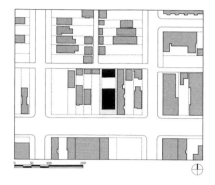

Site Plan

Second Floor Plan

1. Entry
2. Office Reception
3. Office
4. Work Area
5. Conference
6. Living
7. Dining
8. Kitchen
9. Bedroom
10. Dressing

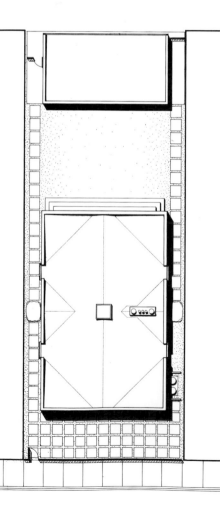

First Floor Plan

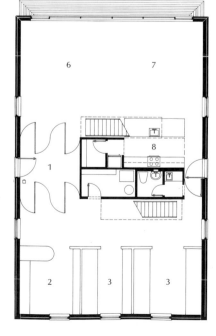

Roof Plan

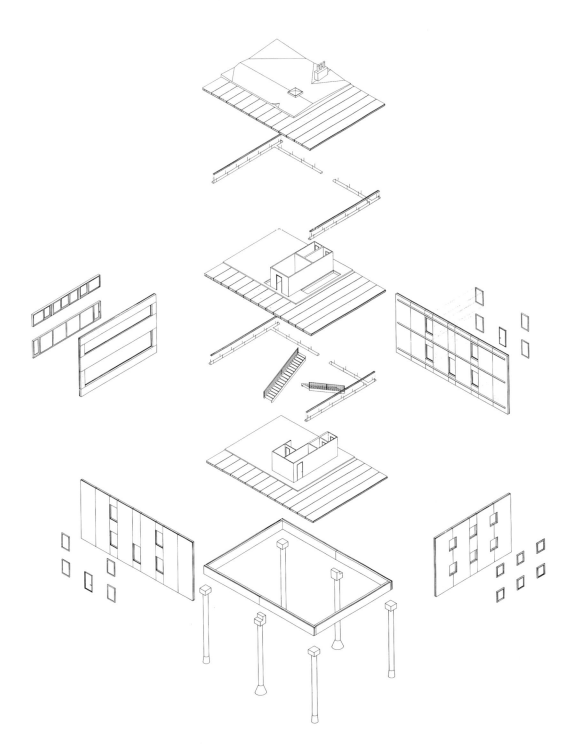

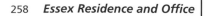

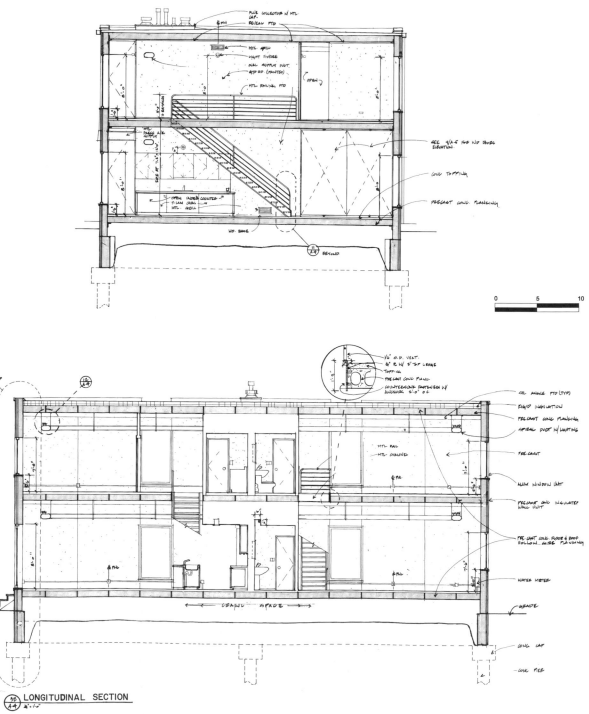

LONGITUDINAL SECTION

House on Deer Isle

Deer Isle, Maine

Peter Forbes & Associates Architects

The extraordinary, but fragile beauty of an ocean-side site led to a design that carefully juxtaposes the constructed object with the natural environment. Uncompromisingly man-made in both its geometry and materials—glass, leaded copper, and cut stone—the house reflects or dissolves into the landscape without compromising its own formal integrity.

The house is composed of two pavilions: master bedroom, and living/dining/kitchen. Each is defined by concrete piers at the corners, which support tubular steel trusses spanning the entire space to carry the laminated cedar roof deck. Exterior walls, free of any load-bearing function, are glass. Massive stone chimneys stand nearly free of the pavilions, visually anchoring the composition to the surrounding ledges.

The program required several subordinate houses for various family members and their guests. Together, these constitute a family of buildings attendant to the glass house, which serves as the parent's dwelling and principal gathering place for meals and social activities. By its siting, the cluster of pavilions directs physical and visual exploration of the site and forms an inner space among the buildings that is manicured, polished, and serene. Beyond the perimeter of this civilized clearing, nature immediately prevails—birch and spruce forest, rocky promontory, and the ocean itself.

Above: *Seen from the sea shore, the house appears to grow out of the rock ledges that form the site. The chimneys are built of native stone, blending into the landscape. The attached pavilions become transparent tents, ephemeral structures reflecting every change in season or weather.*

Opposite Page: *The transparent pavilions form a screen to the magnificent view, controlling the observer's experience in a series of glimpses between columns, trees or chimneys until the moment when each vista is revealed, each enhanced by the sense of anticipation developed by the experience.*

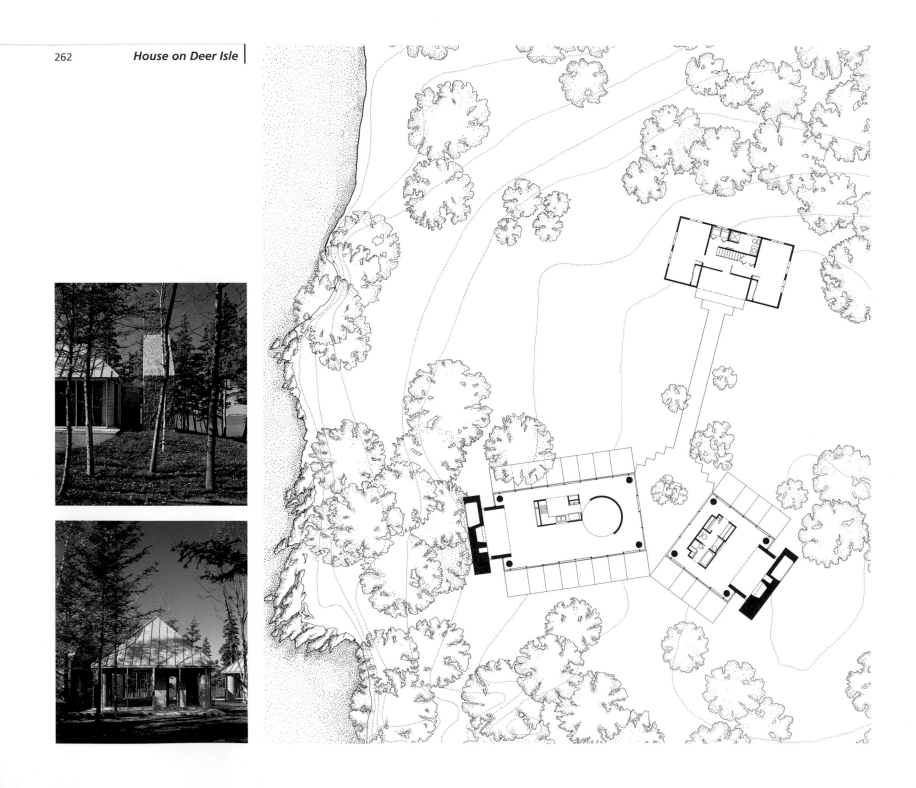

Left: *The most powerful spatial moment in the composition of the three pavilions is the wedge of space between the two glass buildings, as if the air were made more dense by the pressure of the two glass walls being forced apart and the presence of the third pavilion at the end of its stone path. This is the point from which the view of the ocean is ultimately revealed.*

Opposite Page: *The glass pavilions are opened to one another, exchanging reflections and a continuity of space.*

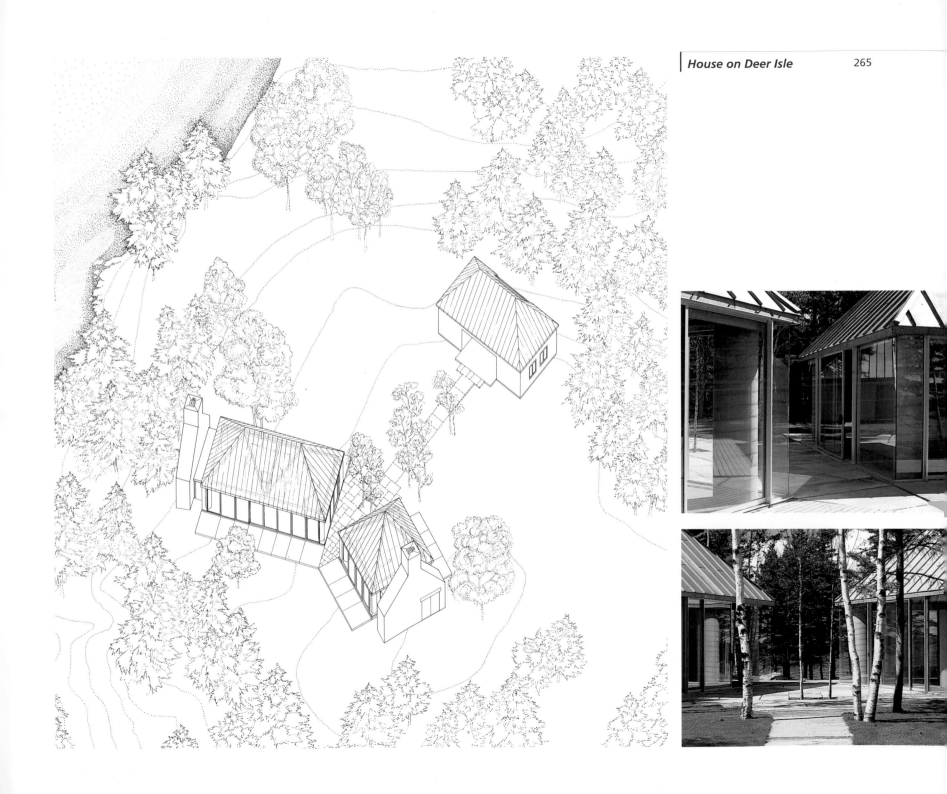

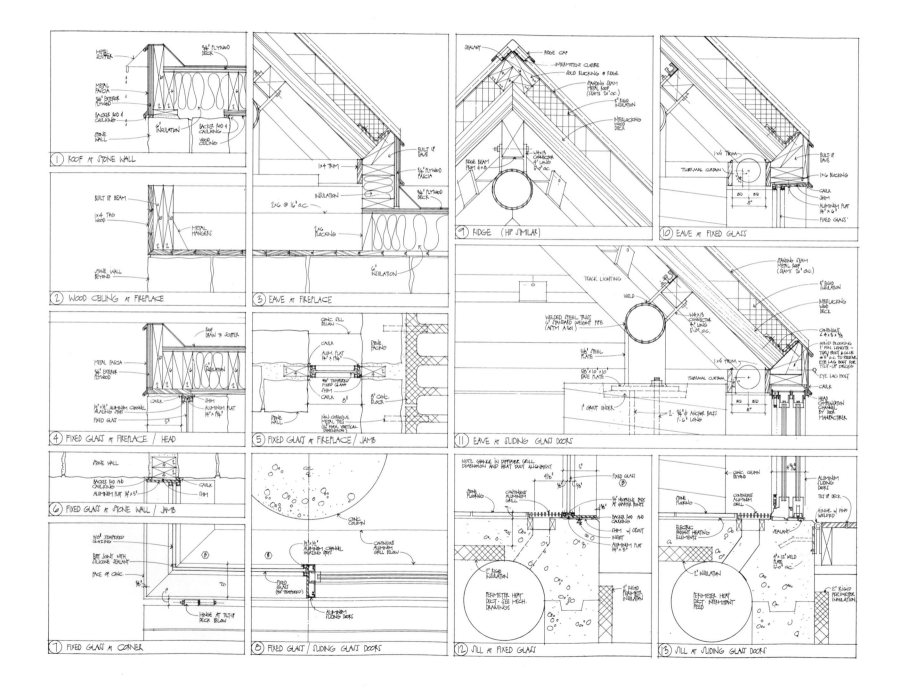

1 ROOF AT STONE WALL

2 WOOD CEILING AT FIREPLACE

3 EAVE AT FIREPLACE

4 FIXED GLASS AT FIREPLACE / HEAD

5 FIXED GLASS AT FIREPLACE / JAMB

6 FIXED GLASS AT STONE WALL / JAMB

7 FIXED GLASS AT CORNER

8 FIXED GLASS / SLIDING GLASS DOORS

9 RIDGE (HIP SIMILAR)

10 EAVE AT FIXED GLASS

11 EAVE AT SLIDING GLASS DOORS

12 SILL AT FIXED GLASS

13 SILL AT SLIDING GLASS DOORS

Above Left: *Where the chimneys penetrate under the pavilion roofs, a deep inglenook is formed, a separate room for the fireplace or, as if the fireplace had become an inhabitable space.*

Left: *Under the tent-like roof structure of steel tubes and cedar planking are separate enclosures for the dining area and the kitchen. The dining area is contained within a curved screen of gray cedar. The kitchen inhabits a separate "house," complete with a window that aligns with a distant island and light house.*

Right: Although both of the principal pavilions are essentially a single room, both achieve a great deal of spatial complexity and excitement from the juxtaposition of the subforms within the rooms.

Opposite Page: The chimneys penetrate to form strong hearth enclosures, the separate "houses" of the kitchen and bathroom describe a sequence of entry, passage, and arrival spaces by their relationship to the exterior glass partition.

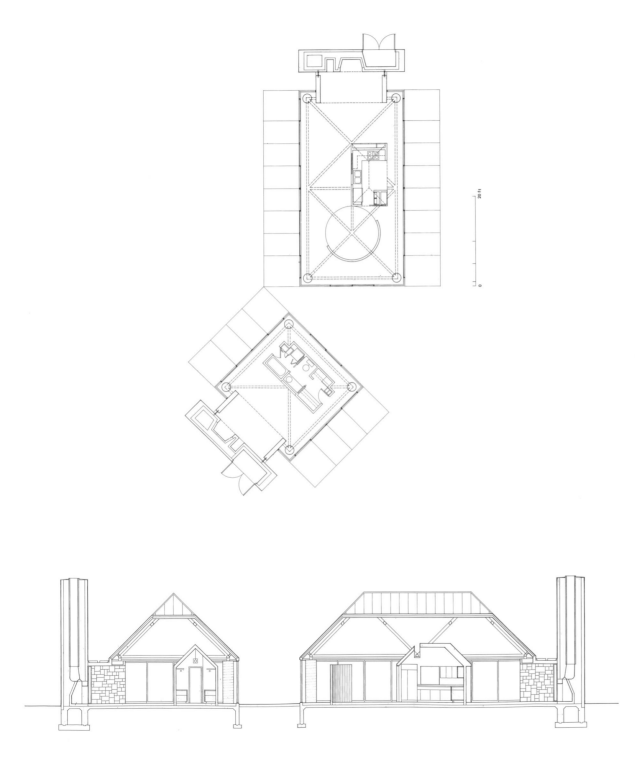

House on Great Cranberry Island

Great Cranberry Island, Maine

Peter Forbes & Associates Architects

Two long, glass-walled pavilions are drawn across this coastal site at the juncture of dense forest and open meadow to strengthen and articulate the natural division of the landscape. At a break between the pavilions, two massive stone chimneys form a gateway, allowing passage from the lush woods to the barren ocean frontage and directing entry into the house.

Divided into family accommodations and guest quarters, the spaces are intentionally very simple in their organization and geometric form in order to frame and set off the remarkable natural setting—on one side, the immediate miniature landscape of rocks and mosses on the forest floor, while on the other the sheer dramatic landscape of sparse grass, black basalt ledges, and the open sea.

Structurally and formally the building is a series of transverse-bearing walls carrying the roof deck. The walls are pierced by large and small openings to provide a continuous sequence of varied spaces. Free of any load-bearing function, the exterior longitudinal walls are entirely sliding glass panels framed in teak and mahogany. All of the interior and exterior surfaces are otherwise of wood—cedar, mahogany, or douglas fir.

Above: Seen from the shore across its open meadow, the house hugs the ground, the roof ridge line below the trees, the entire composition consciously subordinate to the natural condition of the site, but defining the transitions from open space to dense forest, meadow grass to pine woods.

Opposite Page: Beyond Great Cranberry Island there is no other land, no further islands only the open sea. The gateway formed by the stone chimneys directs and frames the view to the ocean, articulating even the distant horizon that would otherwise remain an indefinable expanse.

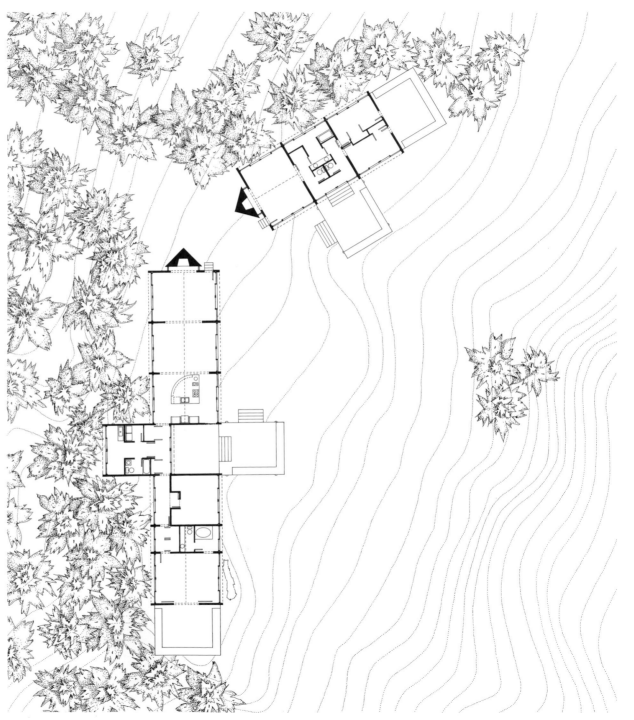

Left: *The two arms of the house align not with the edge of the sea shore, but, rather, with the rock ledges that run obliquely into the sea.*

Opposite Page: *Exposed to extreme ocean weather conditions and often shrouded in fog, the house had to be built to withstand both violent forces and the effects of nearly continuous moisture. Like a boat, the house is built of rot-resistant woods, such as cedar and teak, and lead for weather proofing. Even the chimneys act as stone "ballast," anchoring the wood structure against the force of the wind.*

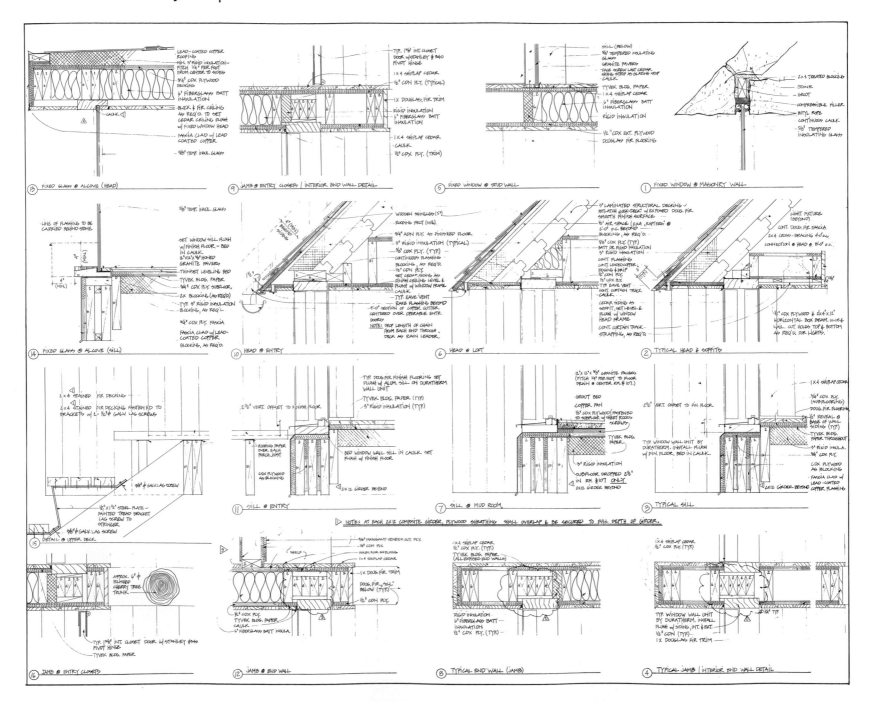

Above Left: *The kitchen, dining room, and living room are each defined by the bearing walls that span the house every sixteen feet. However, the "telescope" effect of each opening getting progressively wider from the chimney to the kitchen connects the spaces by reversing the effects of perspective.*

Left: *An order of materials articulates the structural concept of the house. All structural walls are clad in cedar. All non-structural walls are of mahogany. All spanning materials—roof and floors—are of Douglas fir.*

House on Potomac River

Washington, D.C.
Peter Forbes & Associates Architects

I n an archetypical suburban setting, this house sits in a row of detached single-family houses, all built in the early 1950s, all with nearly identical floor plans, each sited twelve feet from the next along a genuinely beautiful street that overlooks the Potomac River.

Strictly aligned with their property lines, the existing houses face slightly, disturbingly, away from the view. Built through the "ruins" of one of the typical houses, this building corrects the alignment by skewing perpendicular to the river, while incorporating the footprint of the original house with its orderly relationship to the rest of the neighborhood. The vestiges of the original brick walls remain as an entry and kitchen with adjacent courtyards, and continue through the new building as the dining room/stairwell wall.

The new structure is light wood frame with both roof and exterior walls sheathed in lead-coated copper, not dissimilar from many traditional tin-clad Southern buildings. The plan organization itself follows that model—an open-breezeway house oriented to the prevailing summer wind as well as the view. Largely closed to the adjacent neighbors, the house maintains everyone's privacy and acknowledges the scale and pattern of its surroundings.

Above: The simple pewter-colored lead-coated copper walls make a pleasing foil for the patterns of shade and flowering trees that are the most important defining element of the neighborhood.

Opposite Page: Within the context of the suburban neighborhood, the house consciously follows the precedent of simple forms and small scale, while breaking with that tradition to more accurately reflect the realities of neighborliness in a congested living situation.

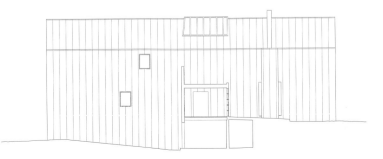

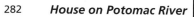

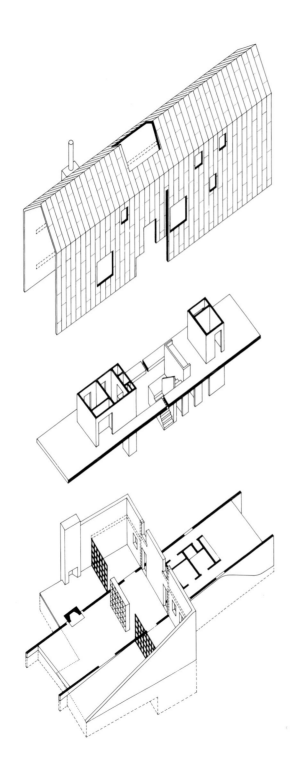

Left: *At the intersection of the two spatial volumes—that formed by the low pre-existing structure and the lofty nave of the new—the space rises unobstructed to the roof and a translucent insulated skylight.*

Opposite Page: *Looking from the entry through the intersection of the new building to the kitchen beyond, the layering of space is articulated by both the materials of each sequential surface and by the different qualities of light in each space.*

House on Mount Desert Island

Mount Desert Island, Maine

Peter Forbes & Associates Architects

Three important concerns of the owner combined to generate the formal order of this house. First, the landscape of the area, both immediate and distant, is essential to the owner's daily experience. Second, natural light and the passage of time—daily and seasonally—are important sources of pleasure to the owner. Third, the owner is acutely allergic to a myriad of substances, both natural and man-made, and cannot be exposed to them for prolonged periods of time.

The formal response to these concerns has been to create an open framework of steel tubes—open to avoid mold and dust accumulation, steel as an inert and non-allergenic material—within which floors and rooms are platforms floating in space. Inside the building the only partitions are to separate bathrooms and closets, and these are of cedar with a water-based stain finish. Since plywood, gypsum wallboard, plaster, and most paints are receptors of molds and generators of toxins, they could not be present in the dwelling. The exterior walls of the living spaces are entirely glass and aluminum.

The open, glass-enclosed space is suffused with light, constantly changing through the course of the day and the year. The steel frame casts its pattern and, in turn, receives the lattice of shadows cast by the window-wall. Similarly, the open, transparent structure dissolves into the landscape—platforms in the forest to observe and experience nature. Rising to forty feet in the trees, the house affords a spectacular view of both the immediate environment and the distant mountains of Acadia National Park.

Above: *Rising in a clearing on the brow of a hill, the house gently commands its site without disturbing the natural surroundings. The land was disturbed as little as possible during construction and replanted with native blueberry and bunchberry sod. A grove of white birch trees has been planted on the same grid as the house structure to mediate the transition from man-made to natural environment.*

Opposite Page: *The elements of the house construction are of a scale in keeping with the trees, rocks, and landforms of the site. This scalar relationship is as important as the transparency of the house in establishing its intimacy with the landscape.*

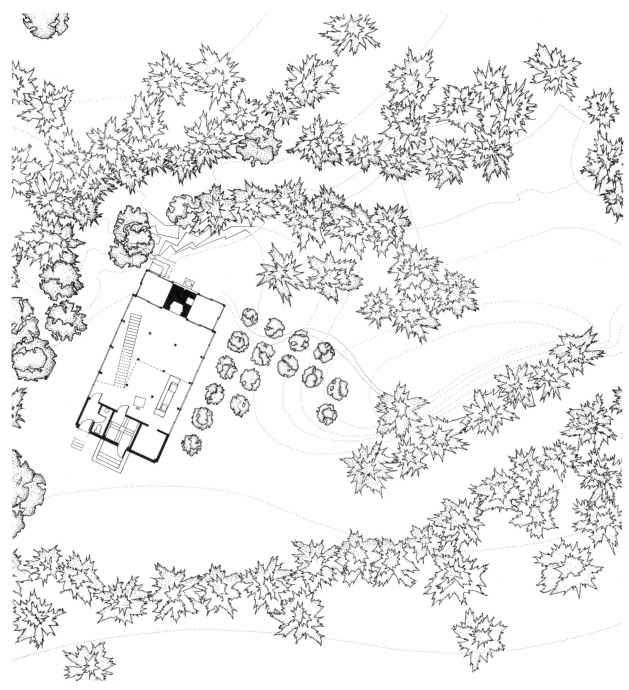

Left: *To effect the transition between land and structure, a set of monumental slabs of rough-cut native granite form the entrance steps. The stainless-steel roof scupper spills into a carved-stone catch-basin.*

Opposite Page: *One of the cubes of space defined by the house grid is occupied by the fireplace, a cube of concrete sculpted to also function as a massive scupper draining the steep metal roof.*

Right: Welded steel tubes satisfy the requirement for a structure that encloses space without interior walls, a requirement dictated by the multiple allergies of the owner and the need to circulate and exchange air without impediment. Within the steel grid, rooms can be platforms hanging in space, separated by space and geometry alone.

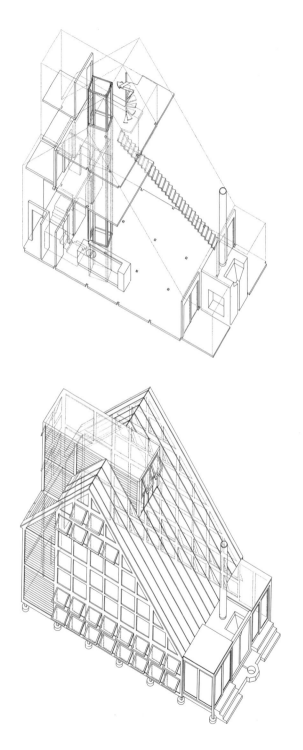

Top: *From the second-level platform, space flows over the cabinetry that forms a parapet, down through the grid cut by the stair, around the structure to join with the space below.*

Center: *On the second level the elevator is enclosed with finely perforated metal screen, which acts like a theater scrim.*

Bottom: *Leaping through the grid at an oblique angle, the main stair establishes a grid for circulation, which is followed by the orientation of the elevator beyond and the spiral stair above.*

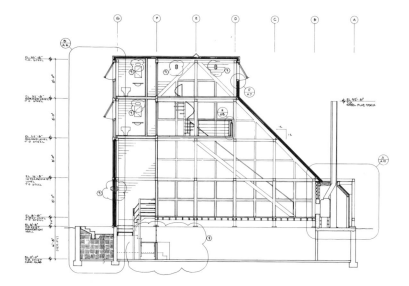

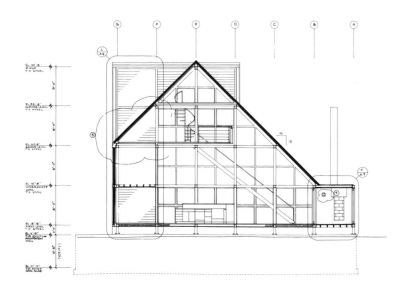

This Page: Although the entire living space is un-partitioned, the strong geometry of the grid defines different living areas within the larger envelope. There is a distinct sense of spatial differentiation in the cube of space by the fireplace, as opposed to the cube of space inhabited by the dining table, even though these two areas are immediately adjacent.

Opposite Page: Seen from the glass elevator rising through the open grid, disconnected from any floor, the prismatic quality of the house is most apparent.

House at Orcutt Harbor

Orcutt Harbor, Maine
Peter Forbes & Associates Architects

Three processions determine the order and form of this house. First, the building form processes across the site, starting at the point of access to the property and extending to the legal setback from the water's edge. The house acts as a formal bridge from the deep woods to the steep rocks of the shore, beginning as a protecting, closed form and gradually unfolding to take advantage of the views.

On a functional level, the house progresses from the enclosed utilitarian demands of garage, shop, and laundry to the private realms of bedrooms, to the open areas of public entertaining. As in the formal procession across the site, this programmatic procession is physically manifested in the gradual dissolution of enclosing walls into glass, the expansion of one's perception from the defined edges of a room to the limitless horizon.

In addition to these formal and functional transitions, there is an historical progression from the archetypal American house to the far more ephemeral, relativistic notion of dwelling in our present, less-structured society. The building begins as a highly traditional gable-end house, firmly anchored to its surroundings, but then it extrudes toward the horizon, accelerating in the frequency and size of its openings, shedding its dormers, enclosing walls and, ultimately, its roof. Finally, the form vibrates into thin air, a composition of pure glass, open rafters, and taut wires scarcely in contact with the ground below. The only hesitation in this accelerating procession is at the slight deformation where the linear form passes the implied force field of the owner's radio transmission tower. This temporary moment of deceleration, emphasized by a circular arrival platform, identifies the formal entrance and establishes a cross axis with the chimney and the hearth within.

Above: *Upon entering the site, the first view of the house is this gable end, highly evocative of traditional New England structures. Only the rigorous elimination of trim and detail reveal its modernist antecedents in addition to its traditional ones.*

Opposite Page: *Turning the corner of the house, its extraordinary length and the gradual dissolution of the form are exposed. As the building accelerates toward the shore, the spacing of solid elements—dormers, the chimney—become less frequent and then disappear completely. Conversely, openings in the fabric of the building—doors, windows, porches— occur more frequently and become larger until the wall and roof dissolve.*

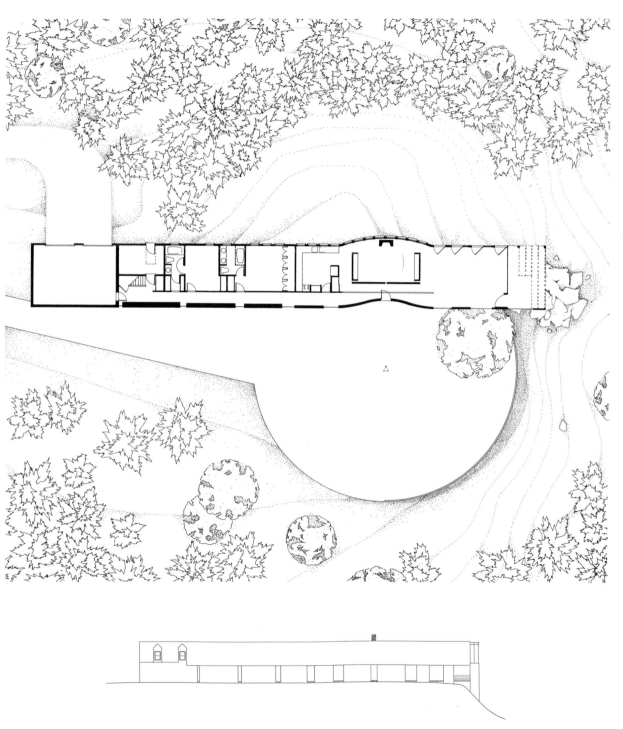

Left: At the ocean end of the house the roof
enclosure dissolves, exposing the naked
rafters, the walls reach their minimum thick-
ness and glass is eliminated from the openings.

Opposite Page: On the north side of the
house, severely minimal openings filled with
fixed glazing proceed toward a horizon formed
by the edge of a steep drop toward the ocean.

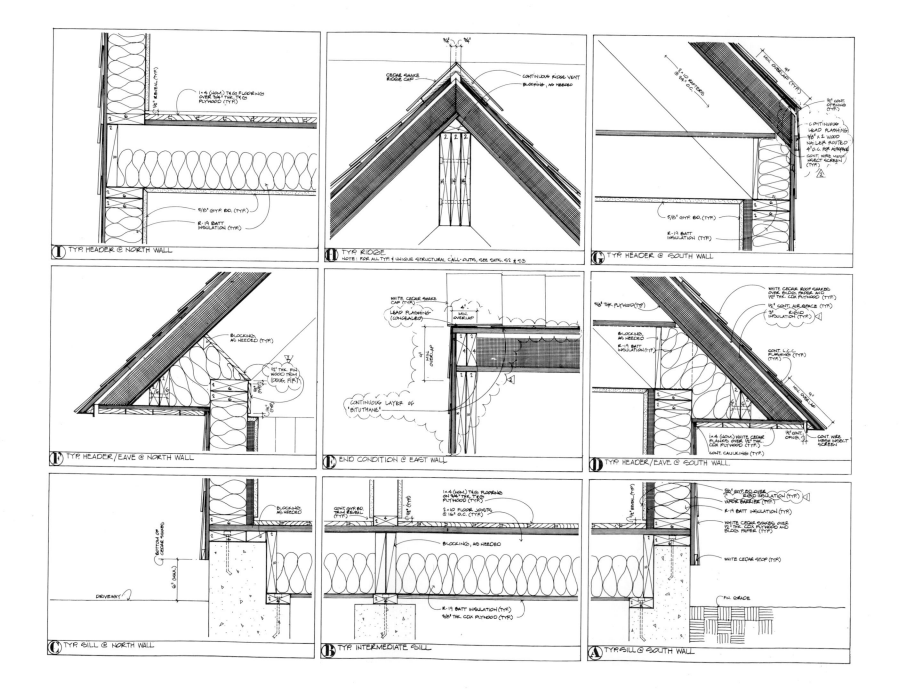

I TYP. HEADER @ NORTH WALL

1x4 (NOM.) T&G FLOORING OVER 3/4" THK. T&G PLYWOOD (TYP.)

5/8" GYP. BD. (TYP.)

R-19 BATT INSULATION (TYP.)

H TYP. RIDGE
NOTE: FOR ALL TYP. & UNIQUE STRUCTURAL CALL-OUTS, SEE SHTS. S2 & S3

CEDAR SHAKE RIDGE CAP

CONTINUOUS RIDGE VENT

BLOCKING, AS NEEDED

G TYP. HEADER @ SOUTH WALL

2x10 RAFTERS @ O.C.

MIN. OVERLAP

1/4" CONT. OPENING (TYP.)

CONTINUOUS LEAD FLASHING 3/8" x 2 WOOD NAILER ROUTED 4' O.C. FOR AIRSPACE

CONT. WIRE MESH INSECT SCREEN (TYP.)

5/8" GYP. BD. (TYP.)

R-19 BATT INSULATION (TYP.)

F TYP. HEADER/EAVE @ NORTH WALL

BLOCKING, AS NEEDED (TYP.)

1/2" THK. FIN. WOOD TRIM (DOUG. FIR)

E END CONDITION @ EAST WALL

WHITE CEDAR SHAKE CAP (TYP.)

LEAD FLASHING (CONCEALED)

MIN. OVERLAP

WALL OVERLAP

R-19 BATT INSULATION (TYP.)

CONTINUOUS LAYER OF "BITUTHANE"

D TYP. HEADER/EAVE @ SOUTH WALL

WHITE CEDAR ROOF SHAKES OVER BLDG. PAPER AND 1/2" THK. CDX PLYWOOD (TYP.)

1/2" CONT. AIRSPACE (TYP.)

3" RIGID INSULATION (TYP.)

5/8" THK. PLYWOOD (TYP.)

BLOCKING, AS NEEDED

R-19 BATT INSULATION (TYP.)

CONT. L.G.C. FLASHING (TYP.)

WALL OVERLAP

1x4 (NOM.) WHITE CEDAR PLANKS OVER 1/2" THK. CDX PLYWOOD (TYP.)

CONT. CAULKING (TYP.)

1/4" CONT. OPENING

CONT. WIRE MESH INSECT SCREEN

C TYP. SILL @ NORTH WALL

BLOCKING, AS NEEDED

BOTTOM OF CEDAR SHAKES

6" (MAX.)

DRIVEWAY

B TYP. INTERMEDIATE SILL

CONT. GYP. BD. TRIM REVEAL (TYP.)

1x4 (NOM.) T&G FLOORING ON 3/4" THK. T&G PLYWOOD (TYP.)

2x10 FLOOR JOISTS @ 16" O.C. (TYP.)

BLOCKING, AS NEEDED

R-19 BATT INSULATION (TYP.)

3/8" THK. CDX PLYWOOD (TYP.)

A TYP. SILL @ SOUTH WALL

5/8" GYP. BD. OVER RIGID INSULATION (TYP.)

R-19 BATT INSULATION (TYP.)

WHITE CEDAR SHAKES OVER 1/2" THK. CDX PLYWOOD AND BLDG. PAPER (TYP.)

WHITE CEDAR STOP (TYP.)

FIN. GRADE

Right: *Along the north side of the house a corridor connects the various private living spaces, ultimately opening into the more public living/dining room. The exterior wall of this corridor becomes progressively thinner at each window opening.*

Opposite Page: *To a height of eight feet the interior finish of the house is highly refined. Above the eight foot level, the muscular structure of the roof is revealed. The structure of Douglas fir rafters ripples and flexes to accommodate the sensuous curves of the building.*

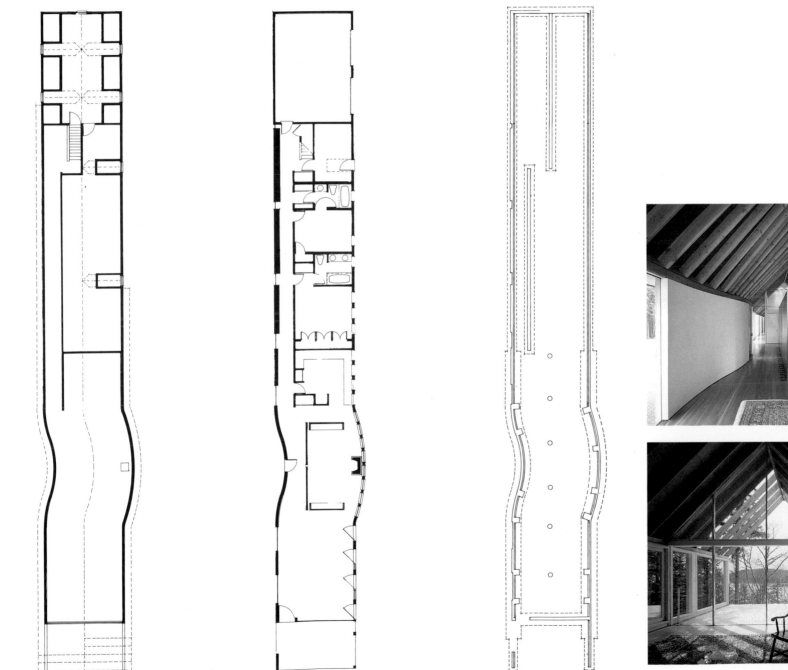

House in Surry

Surry, Maine

Peter Forbes & Associates Architects

L andscape, geometry, and light interact to define this seaside dwelling. The program was for a retirement home and studio of a couple with a large extended family who would all come to visit during the summer. The owners have a lifetime of belongings, but a desire for uncluttered spaces and room to display their art. Hence, the open plan needed to be served by extensive storage space contained in a series of pods or "saddlebags" clipped onto the inland side of the house. The resultant principal living space, free of support services or structure, is a lofty room, 58 feet long, terminating in a massive chimney wall of cut local granite.

The site is a meadow with few trees, a broad pebble beach, and spectacular views of Blue Hill Bay and Mt. Desert Island. As this is a flood-plain area, regulation required the house to be built up off the ground with concrete piers to support the floor. These piers, extended up to eave height, carry the roof as well and establish an order of paired columns that bends and shifts to accommodate the landscape. To the columns are clipped steel beams and rafters, creating a continuous pavilion that floats above the ground. Within this ordered structure, storage elements, enclosed sleeping areas, folding decks, kitchen, and baths are inserted as free-standing objects wrapped or interposed with glass.

The open site is suffused with intense, un-shaded light, magnified further by reflection from the water scarcely 25 yards away. The light surrounds each component of the architecture, articulating the parts, dissolving the structural fabric, and creating an elusive, palpitant, mirage-like form.

Above: The end elevation reveals the basic structure of the house repeated at each bay, every sixteen feet for the length of the building. A pair of columns rise from the ground to carry, first, paired steel beams at floor level, and then extend to eave height to bear a composite roof structure of steel angle rafters infilled with wood panels.

Opposite Page: At the minimum allowed distance from the ocean, the house hinges at its mid-point to follow and embrace the curve of the shore. Located in a flood plain district, the house was required by regulation to be built above ground level.

Above: *Free from any load-bearing require-ments, the envelope of the house can be entirely glass. Expressed at each corner, glass meets glass in a minimalist transparent joint, sharply contrasting with the sturdy structural column outside it.*

Opposite Page: *At the moment where the building opens, the "hinge," a single column bears both pavilion roofs. The roofs nearly touch at this apex, clearly articulating the implied continuity of structure from one pavil-ion to the next.*

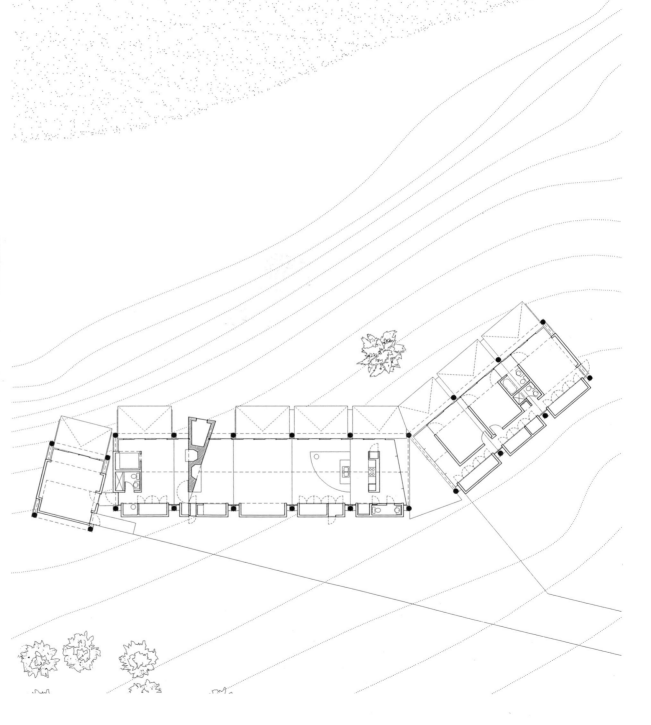

Right: *The public and private realms of the main house are divided by the granite chimney. On the near side is a great room encompassing living, dining, and kitchen. Beyond the chimney is the master bedroom and bath.*

Opposite Page: *Along the inland side of the entire house are a series of prefabricated modules, which contain storage, bathrooms, laundry facilities, pantry, and the like. A continuous ribbon of clerestory window runs above the modules, interspersed at each column with floor-to-ceiling operable windows.*

Marquand Retreat

Naches River Valley, Washington

Miller Hull Partnership Architects

The Naches River west of Yakima flows from the Cascade Mountains to the east and has carved out a beautiful valley rimmed by basalt cliffs. Attracted to the arid climate, the client, a busy Seattle publisher, purchased a 200-acre (81-hectare) "bowl" on the slope of a mountain. The site faces down into the river valley and cliffs beyond, and is used for weekend getaways. The owner set the design challenge: to construct a limited, two-room program using materials that were resistant to fire, wind, and intruders. The design had to respond to the potential for both blistering heat and freezing cold. However, the owner still wanted natural light and an architecture that expressed the raw quality of the site.

The structure was conceived as a thin metal roof floated across a basic concrete block rectangle. The floating roof provides a shaded porch to the south, clerestory window slots at the main shell, and a covered path out to the water cistern tower to the rear of the building. A ten-foot- (three-meter-) square opening faces south under the porch with two full-size sliding doors hung on a track running the entire length of the wall. With one door screened and one glazed, the owner can customize the proportion of open ventilation to glazed area. The material palette consists of concrete block, and structural wood decking with metal roofing and wood windows. Since the 450-square-foot (42-square-meter) structure lacks permanent power, a wood stove effectively provides heat. The cistern is currently filled by a water truck, with plans for a well to be dug in the future .

Above: *Small "punched" openings in the east and west walls capture select views of the site while being easily protected when the cabin is unoccupied.*

Opposite Page: *The sturdy structure sits stoically within the basalt-rimmed desert valley in eastern Washington State.*

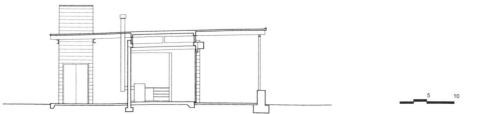

Section Facing East

5   10

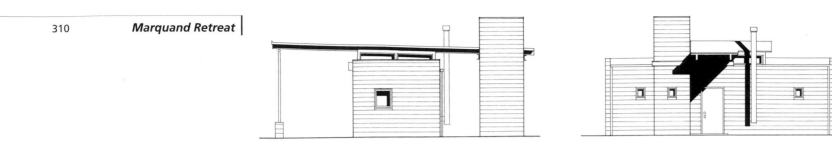

East Elevation

North Elevation

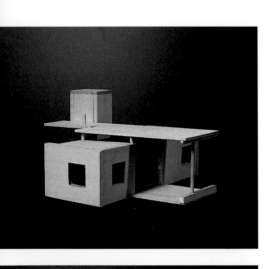

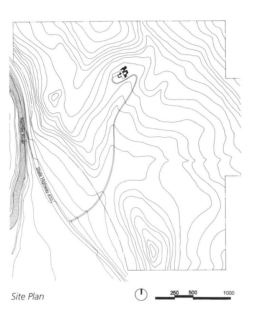

Site Plan

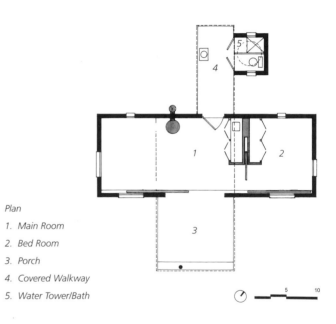

Plan

1. Main Room

2. Bed Room

3. Porch

4. Covered Walkway

5. Water Tower/Bath

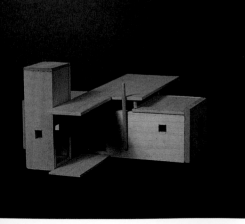

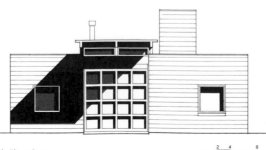

South Elevation

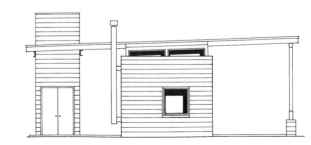

West Elevation

This Page: All the openings are operable for natural light and ventilation in this variable and harsh climate, and all can be closed off against weather and intruders when the building is empty.

Opposite Page: The project is an exercise in elemental forms that suit their purpose—a tower bath and cistern, a box for living, and a simple plane roof with one column for shelter.

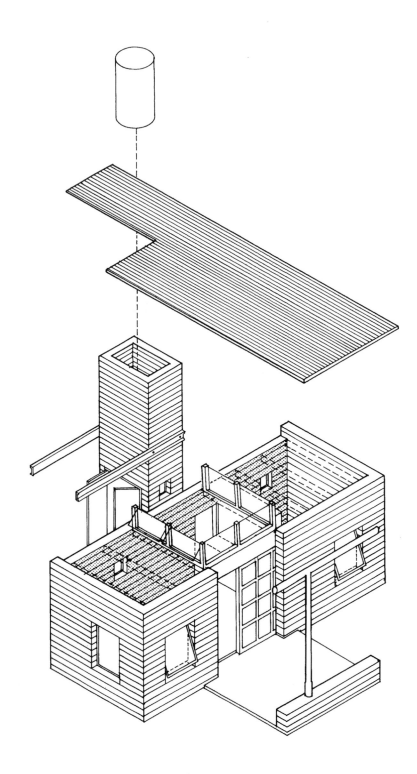

This Page: *Twin doors of glass and screen on a single track allow the occupant to modulate the proportion of ventilation to suit conditions.*

Opposite Page: *Kept small, the punched windows maximize the mass of the concrete masonry walls. The sliding doors slip over and are seen through the small front windows from the exterior.*

Campbell Residence

Yakima Valley, Washington

Miller Hull Partnership Architects

The site for this home is an 180-acre (73-hectare) ranch at the base of the Cascade Mountain foothills near the small town of Tieton, Washington. At 1800 feet (549 meters) in elevation, the ranch sits on a plateau, with dramatic views west to the mountains and east to the Naches River Valley. The owners, who currently reside in San Anselmo, California, are third-generation owners of this seventy-five-year-old ranch and orchard; they plan to eventually relocate to the Seattle area. Their desires for the home were twofold: to provide a home base for regular trips to the ranch, and eventually to serve as a second home for extended stays. Prevailing wind was a primary factor in the design of the home, influencing the decision to tuck the house into a hillside for shelter. Further wind protection is gained by the construction of a wall at one end of an open carport, with a large sliding door to access the house or shut out the wind. The wall also provides security, as the owners are absent for much of the time.

The house is split into three primary pieces—the carport and wind protection wall; a small office; and the main house. The outdoor space, framed between the building elements and a large existing ponderosa pine, is the focus of the house. One of the owners, an interior designer, provided immaculately detailed custom cabinetry and fixtures throughout the project.

The building materials are rugged: concrete block walls, used to hold back the hillside, are exposed inside and out. Recycled Douglas fir purlins are set on exposed steel beams and columns that are canted to mimic the old orchard props used to support fruit-laden branches. Indoor and outdoor space are connected by a stained concrete slab which extends out and engages basalt boulders found on the site.

Campbell Residence

1. Carport
2. Office
3. Living/Dining
4. Kitchen
5. Bath
6. Mech./Storage
7. Master Bedroom

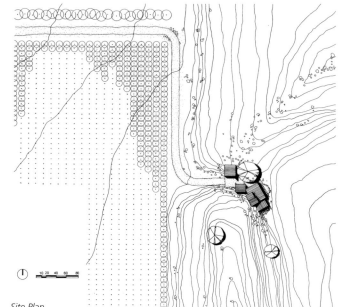

Site Plan

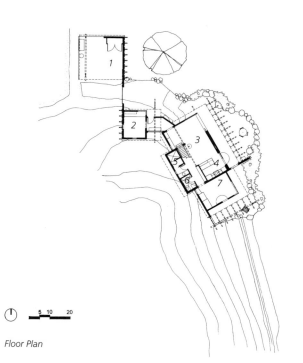

Floor Plan

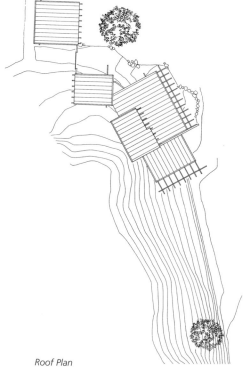

Roof Plan

Left: *The camp-like arrangement of building elements is spread within the site to frame and shelter outdoor rooms within the vast landscape.*

Opposite Page: *The house unfolds as it wraps along the hillside, terminating in the outdoor terrace space off the master bedroom.*

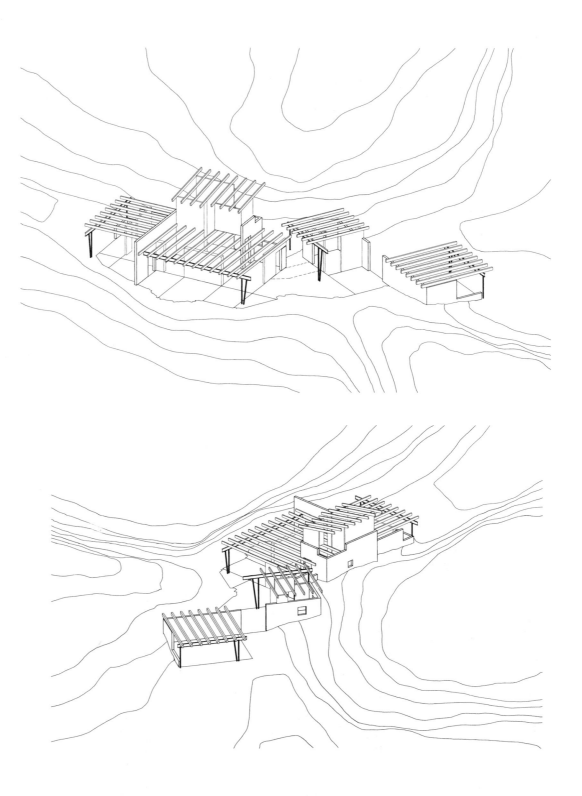

Right: Each building element was placed in response to the setting, framing a variety of dramatic views.

Opposite Page: Careful detailing further emphasizes the tectonic attributes of the building.

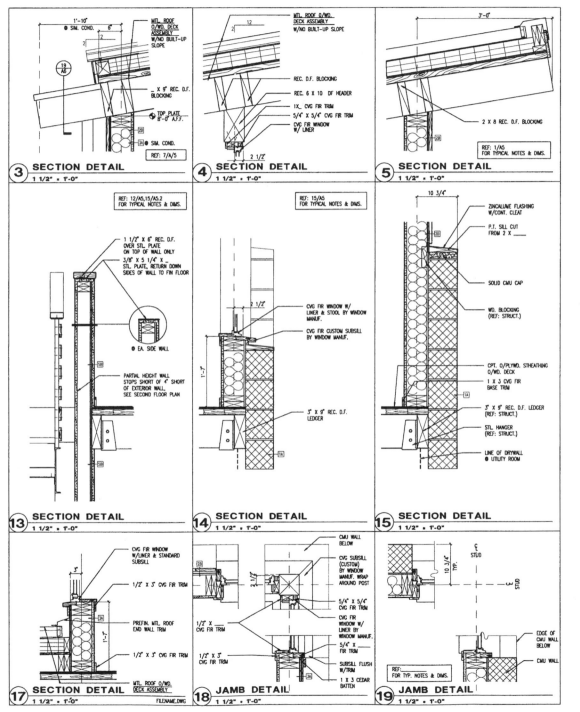

Detail 3 — SECTION DETAIL (1 1/2" = 1'-0")
- 1'-10" @ SIM. COND.
- 6"
- MTL. ROOF O/WD. DECK ASSEMBLY W/NO BUILT-UP SLOPE
- _ X 9" REC. D.F. BLOCKING
- 19/A5
- TOP PLATE 8'-0" A.F.F.
- SIM. COND.
- REF: 7/A/5

Detail 4 — SECTION DETAIL (1 1/2" = 1'-0")
- MTL. ROOF O/WD. DECK ASSEMBLY W/NO BUILT-UP SLOPE
- 12
- REC. D.F. BLOCKING
- REC. 6 X 10 DF HEADER
- 1X_ CVG FIR TRIM
- 5/4" X 5/4" CVG FIR TRIM
- CVG FIR WINDOW W/ LINER
- 2 1/2"

Detail 5 — SECTION DETAIL (1 1/2" = 1'-0")
- 3'-0"
- 2 X 8 REC. D.F. BLOCKING
- REF: 1/A5 FOR TYPICAL NOTES & DIMS.

Detail 13 — SECTION DETAIL (1 1/2" = 1'-0")
- REF: 12/A5,15/A5.2 FOR TYPICAL NOTES & DIMS.
- 1 1/2" X 6" REC. D.F. OVER STL PLATE ON TOP OF WALL ONLY
- 3/8" X 5 1/4" X _ STL PLATE, RETURN DOWN SIDES OF WALL TO FIN FLOOR
- @ EA. SIDE WALL
- PARTIAL HEIGHT WALL STOPS SHORT OF 4" SHORT OF EXTERIOR WALL, SEE SECOND FLOOR PLAN

Detail 14 — SECTION DETAIL (1 1/2" = 1'-0")
- REF: 15/A5 FOR TYPICAL NOTES & DIMS.
- 2 1/2"
- 1'-7"
- CVG FIR WINDOW W/ LINER & STOOL BY WINDOW MANUF.
- CVG FIR CUSTOM SUBSILL BY WINDOW MANUF.
- 3" X 9" REC. D.F. LEDGER

Detail 15 — SECTION DETAIL (1 1/2" = 1'-0")
- 10 3/4"
- ZINCALUME FLASHING W/CONT. CLEAT
- P.T. SILL CUT FROM 2 X ___
- SOLID CMU CAP
- WD. BLOCKING (REF: STRUCT.)
- CPT. O/PLYWD. STHEATHING O/WD. DECK
- 1 X 3 CVG FIR BASE TRIM
- 3" X 9" REC. D.F. LEDGER (REF: STRUCT.)
- STL. HANGER (REF: STRUCT.)
- LINE OF DRYWALL @ UTILITY ROOM

Detail 17 — SECTION DETAIL (1 1/2" = 1'-0")
- 3"
- 1'-7"
- CVG FIR WINDOW W/LINER & STANDARD SUBSILL
- 1/2" X 3" CVG FIR TRIM
- PREFIN. MTL. ROOF END WALL TRIM
- 1/2" X 3" CVG FIR TRIM
- MTL. ROOF O/WD. DECK ASSEMBLY
- FILENAME.DWG

Detail 18 — JAMB DETAIL (1 1/2" = 1'-0")
- CMU WALL BELOW
- CVG SUBSILL (CUSTOM) BY WINDOW MANUF. WRAP AROUND POST
- 2 1/2"
- 5/4" X 5/4" CVG FIR TRIM
- CVG FIR WINDOW W/ LINER BY WINDOW MANUF.
- 1/2" X _ CVG FIR TRIM
- 1/2" X 3" CVG FIR TRIM
- 5/4" X _ FIR TRIM
- SUBSILL FLUSH W/TRIM
- 1 X 3 CEDAR BATTEN

Detail 19 — JAMB DETAIL (1 1/2" = 1'-0")
- 10 3/4" TYP.
- 3" STUD
- 3" STUD
- EDGE OF CMU WALL BELOW
- CMU WALL
- REF: FOR TYP. NOTES & DIMS.

Michaels/Sisson Residence

Mercer Island, Washington

Miller Hull Partnership Architects

Situated on a steeply sloping, wooded site alongside a small stream, this residence includes two main stories above a two-story concrete block base containing service spaces. An industrial palette of materials—steel, concrete block, and metal siding—were chosen not only for aesthetic appeal, but also for ease of maintenance.

The concrete block base acts structurally as a stiffened box to retain a fifteen-foot (five-meter) cut into the steep site. The box raises the main living spaces up off the forest floor to increase access to light and air. An expressed steel moment-frame with large wood windows maximizes views into all levels of the forest. One bay of the four-square moment-frame contains a large vertical lift door that opens the house to the site, blurring the boundary between inside and out. At that point, a deck connects the house to the steep hill, providing a level outdoor platform among the trees.

An entry stair tower alongside the garage is cantilevered to prevent damage to the roots of existing Douglas fir trees on the site. This stair leads visitors past the first floor which contains two children's bedrooms, a bathroom, a small play area, laundry, and mechanical storage. As one continues up the stairs, the landing widens to provide space for a small computer area outside of the path of circulation. The upper two stories cantilever off the lower-level garage and bedrooms in an effort to minimize the building footprint on the site. Large sliding panels in the main spaces open up rooms to each other and the outside, creating the feel of an area larger than actually is contained, and forming a living space within the trees.

__Above:__ The upper two stories cantilever off the lower level garage and bedrooms in an effort to minimize the building footprint on the site. On the main level, the kitchen, living, and dining areas open onto a deck with an expansive view of the wooded ravine.

__Opposite Page.__ The entry stair leads visitors past the first floor, which contains mechanical storage, a bathroom, laundry, two purposefully cubby-like children's bedrooms to be completed with built-in furniture and a small play area.

1. Children's Room
2. Bath
3. Playroom
4. Laundry
5. Entry
6. Living
7. Dining
8. Kitchen
9. Music Room
10. Master Bedroom
11. Study

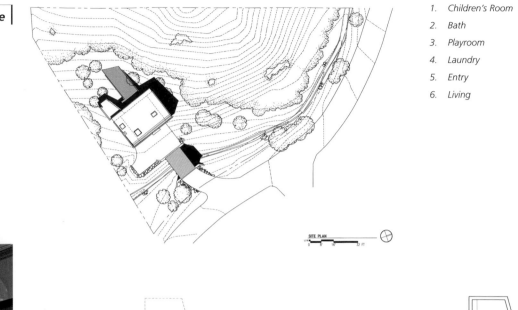

SITE PLAN

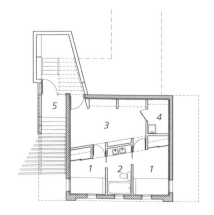

Garage Plan

Second Floor Plan

First Floor Plan

Third Floor Plan

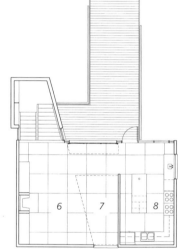

Right: *Pressed-fiber flooring panels, prefabricated cabinets, conduit railing cables, exposed slabs and other low-maintenance materials are used for many interior finishes. The upper floor contains space for a music studio and connects to the master bedroom via a bridge overlooking the living space below.*

Opposite Page: *To maintain privacy, the majority of windows face the front and back of the property rather than the neighbors. Large sliding panels in the main spaces open up rooms to each other and the large vertical lift door opens the house to the back deck.*

Opel Residence

Shelburne, Vermont
Gwathmey Siegel & Associates Architects

A twelve-acre wooded site within the historic Shelburne Farms estate is the bucolic setting for a year-round vacation home built for three generations of the Opel family. Four distinct volumes—a bunkhouse that sleeps eight children, two guesthouses, and the main house—are distributed along a spine, forming a series of indoor and outdoor rooms facing Lake Champlain and the Adirondacks. The development of the house as a "village street" creates a series of private retreats among generous spaces for family gatherings.

From the autocourt, in a grove of maples at the southern end of the house, a covered arcade leads past the bunkhouse stairs and a poolside terrace. As it continues along the closed wall of the guesthouses and their terraces, the arcade opens up to the woods and tennis court to the east, generating a sense of anticipation as the view of the lake is first denied and then revealed again upon entering each of the houses.

A fireplace in a glass wall is the interior focus of the two-and-a-half story vaulted living room in the main house. Sliding glass doors extend the living space onto a large terrace overlooking the lake. The breakfast room flows out from the kitchen, forming the southern "wall" of this outdoor room and providing a private deck for the master bedroom above. From the entrance hall, stairs lead up a half-level to a skylit painter's studio in the east wing, and then up again to the master bedroom that looks out towards the lake, and in across the living room to a round window on the north wall, high under the curve of the vault.

The two smaller guesthouses are identical and are variations on the formal strategies of the main house. The vaulted, double-height living spaces each include a sitting area by the fireplace and a small dining area. Sleeping lofts above the kitchens extend back to create the roof over the arcade. Windows high on the south walls bring light into the living rooms; glazed doors in the north walls lead to recessed terraces, giving each house a private outdoor space with views of the lake.

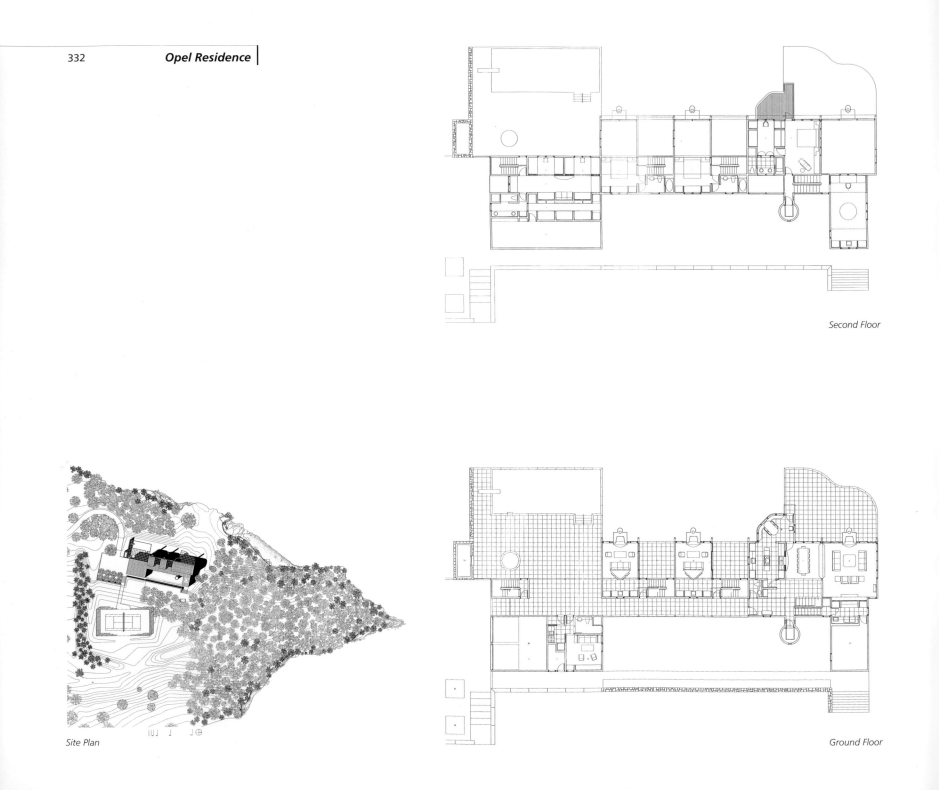

Second Floor

Site Plan

Ground Floor

Prior to the Opel residence, space was treated as a series of opaque and transparent layers within a frame. Here, however, the house is developed as a series of objects on a spine, with a more plastic handling of weight and mass. The curves of the roofs become silhouettes as well as sculptural elements in the building's composition; the malleability and soft reflectiveness of their lead-coated surfaces stand in contrast to the house's vertical cedar siding. The deep, square niches of the guest terraces are counterbalanced by the extruded forms of the main terrace and breakfast room. Three identical stucco fireboxes penetrate the glazed walls of the living rooms, their chimneys rising up as freestanding objects to create a complex and rhythmic juxtaposition of solids and voids.

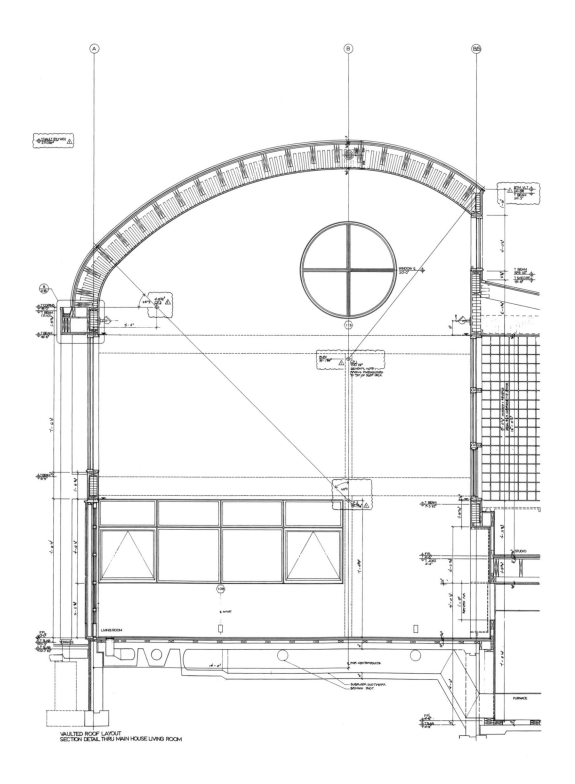

VAULTED ROOF LAYOUT
SECTION DETAIL THRU MAIN HOUSE LIVING ROOM

Left: *The roof vault is a composite curve constructed from three different centerpoints and radii. The modulated shape responds to differing end conditions: the vertical plane of the clerestory window and the horizontal plane of the gutter. The curve extends past the centerline of the circular window, implying closure and creating a complex silhouette rather than a pure geometric segment.*

Bechtler Residence

Zumikon, Switzerland

Gwathmey Siegel & Associates Architects

The 27,000-square-foot sloped site of the Bechtler house is located in the town of Zumikon, northeast of Zurich, and affords dramatic views of the Zurichsee and the Alps to the south, and of hillside pastures to the east and north. Swiss zoning laws require that a strict relationship be maintained between the topography of the site and the height of any proposed building, and the parti responds directly to this context. The formal elements of the house are organized as a cluster of interconnected parts whose overlapping fragments evoke images of a rural village that has been built up over time. These planes and volumes are carved into the hillside as a series of terraces, roof terraces, and roof silhouettes, creating a building whose section is literally derived from the slope of the site.

The owners are patrons of the arts who required a separate gallery space to display their significant collection of contemporary painting and sculpture; extensive areas for public entertaining; and privacy for a family of six children. A double-height entry hall provides access from the autocourt to a two-story spine that forms the north-south axis of the house. A line of smooth concrete columns defines the edge of the painting and sculpture gallery on the ground floor and a dining room, which seats 24, above. The other common areas of the house are grouped on the second level, in three distinct volumes at either end of the spine: the kitchen and breakfast room in the south wing; the three-story living room in the north wing; and the library and music room in a glazed cylinder that steps up a quarter-level to overlook the dining area. The living and dining room face a terraced sculpture garden that acts as an outdoor room, complementing the interior public spaces.

A second stair at the north end of the spine extends the full height of the house and accesses the private areas on the third and fourth levels. In the glazed cylinder above the music room, a 180-degree sweep of windows in the master bedroom reveals a panorama of the Alps to the south. A displaced fragment of the cylinder overlooks the living room to the east, forming a private study. The three-level children's "house" is in the northern and uppermost layer of the site, behind

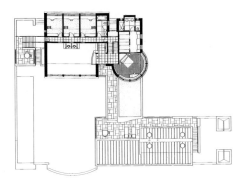

Third Level

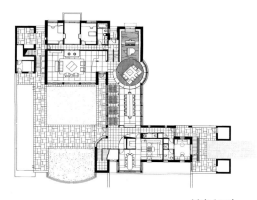

Main Level

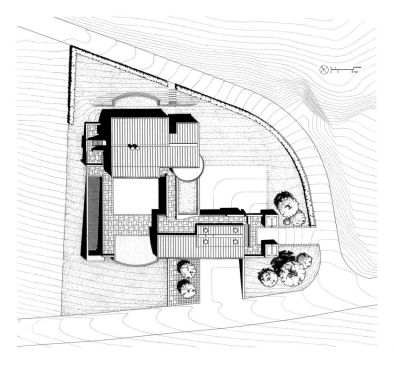

Site Plan

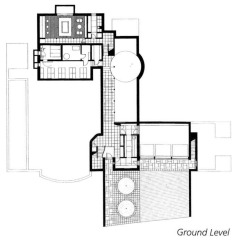

Ground Level

Above: An outdoor stair adjacent to the service entrance leads down one level to the autocourt and up to a roof terrace that connects with the cylindrical master bedroom.

Below: The recessed green limestone wall of the kitchen floats above the garage doors, marking the main entrance from the street. The pattern of the concrete formwork expresses the grid used to organize the house in plan and section, and creates a reveal that conceals the joint between concrete pours.

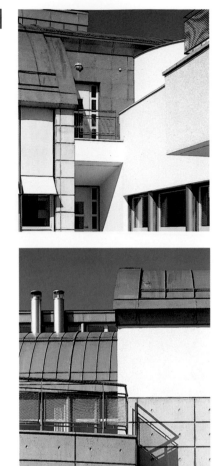

This Page: *The exterior building materials are divided into three horizontal layers: reinforced concrete at the base, stucco upper walls, and lead-coated standing seam roofs. These elements are juxtaposed as the two- and three-story volumes of the house engage the slope of the hill.*

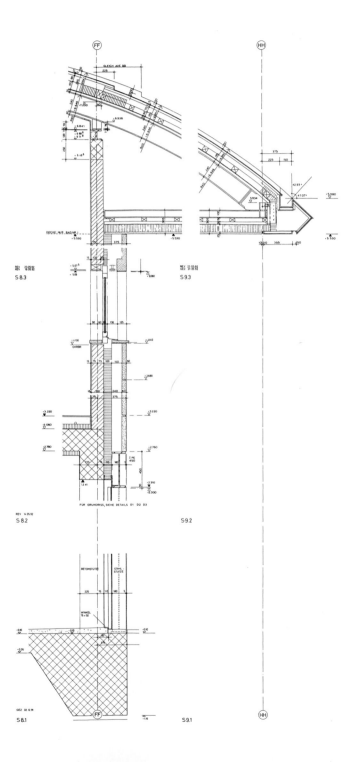

Left: *Expanded metal panels are inset in a stainless steel tubular framework on the interior and exterior handrails, creating a counterpoint between their transparent planes and the dense, material presence of the stone, concrete, and stucco.*

Right: Custom high-intensity light fixtures between the fireplace flues were designed to illuminate the upper edge of the three-story living room ceiling. Recessed track lights along the reveal in the curve of the plaster ceiling can be directed towards specific artworks, such as Richard Long's mud mural on the end wall.

the living room. Bedrooms for the girls are a half-level below the parents' bedroom, and overlook the playroom. The boys' rooms are a half-level above, their loft beds tucked high under the curve of the roof. This arrangement affords a sense of privacy and independence while maintaining a feeling of connection between parents' and children's living spaces.

The Zumikon house offered an opportunity to explore the use of cast-in-place concrete, a common regional technology and craft, in a residential context. The dense, physical presence of the concrete reinforces the impression that the house has been carved out of the site. Exterior walls are finished in white stucco and panels of green German limestone, a material that is repeated in the interior in flooring and countertops. The stainless steel of the curved roofs and external stairs is used again in the interior stair details, the dining room ceiling, and the kitchen cabinets and appliances, reinforcing the interplay between indoor and outdoor "rooms."

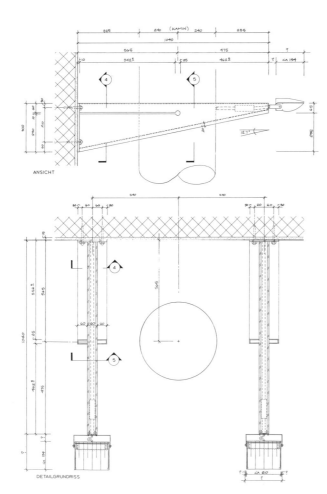

ANSICHT

DETAILGRUNDRISS

Project Credits

Moore House
Site: 5 acres (2 hectares)
Building: 2,400 sq. ft. (216 sq. mt.)
Date of Design: 1986
Construction completed: 1989

House in San Martin
Site: 2 Acres (0.8 hectares)
Building: 800 sq. ft. (74 sq. mt.)
Date of Design: 1983
Construction completed: 1983

House in Gorriti Street
Site: 4,000 sq. ft. (372 sq. mt.)
Building: 2,400 sq. ft. (223 sq. mt.)
Date of Design: 1990
Construction completed: 1991

House in Carranza Street
Site: 4,400 sq. ft. (409 sq. mt.)
Building: 1,800 sq. ft. (167 sq. mt.)
Date of Design: 1994
Construction completed: 1994

House on Paul Harris
Assistant Architects: Ricardo Judson,
Manuel Claro, Ricardo Cruz
Structural Engineer: Rodrigo Mujica
Site: 23,333 sq. ft. (2,100 sq. mt.)
Building: 4,444 sq. ft. (400 sq. mt.)
Date of Design: 1980
Construction completed: 1982

Snail House
Assistant Architects: Jorge Campos, Ricardo Cruz
Structural Engineer: Harmut Vogel
and Rodrigo Mujica
Site: 9,000 sq. ft. (810 sq. mt.)
Building: 2,866 sq. ft. (258 sq. mt.)
Date of Design: 1985
Construction completed: 1987

Garcia House
Architect: Christian DeGroote
Associate Architect: Hugo Molina
Structural Engineering: Luis Soler & Associates
Site: 33,600 sq. ft. (3,125 sq. mt.)
Building: 6,030 sq. ft. (560 sq. mt.)
Date of Design: 1981
Construction completed: 1982

Constanza Vergara House
Architect: Christian DeGroote
Associate Architect: Hugo Molina
Structural Engineering: Luis Soler & Associates
Site: 4,736 sq. ft. (440 sq. mt.)
Building: 2,700 sq. ft. (250 sq. mt.)
Date of Design: 1980
Construction completed: 1981

Matte House
Architect: Christian DeGroote
Associate Architect: Hugo Molina
Structural Engineering: Luis Soler & Associates
Site: 54,250 sq. ft. (5,040 sq. mt.)
Building: 4,725 sq. ft. (439 sq. mt.)
Date of Design: 1986
Construction completed: 1987

Orrego House
Architect: Christian DeGroote
Associate Architect: Hugo Molina
Structural Engineering: Luis Soler & Associates
Site: 95,000 sq. ft. (8,829 sq. mt.)
Building: 3,850 sq. ft. (357 sq. mt.)
Date of Design: 1988
Construction completed: 1989

Elisa House
Architect: Christian DeGroote
Associate Architect: Camila del Fierro
Structural Engineering: Luis Soler & Associates
Site: 64,600 sq. ft. (6,000 sq. mt.)
Building: 10,400 sq. ft. (967 sq. mt.)
Date of Design: 1988
Construction completed: 1990

La Cumbre House
Architect: Christian DeGroote
Associate Architect: Camila del Fierro
Structural Engineering: Jorge Barthou
Site: 12,500 sq. ft. (1,159 sq. mt.)
Building: 3,400 sq. ft. (315 sq. mt.)
Date of Design: 1991
Construction completed: 1993

Errazuriz House
Architect: Christian DeGroote
Associate Architect: Berta Errazuriz
Structural Engineering: Luis Soler & Associates
Site: 247 acre (100 hectares)
Building: 6,000 sq. ft. (550 sq. mt.)
Date of Design: 1991
Construction completed: 1993

The "El Condor" Group
Fajnzylber House
Architect: Christian DeGroote
Associate Architect: Camila del Fierro
Structural Engineering: Luis Soler & Associates
Site: 10,800 sq. ft. (1,000 sq. mt.)
Building: 2,800 sq. ft. (259 sq. mt.)
Date of Design: 1987
Construction completed: 1989

El Condor House
Architect: Christian DeGroote
Associate Architect: Camila del Fierro
Structural Engineering: Luis Soler & Associates
Site: 15,070 sq. ft. (1,400 sq. mt.)
Building: 4,850 sq. ft. (450 sq. mt.)
Date of Design: 1988
Construction completed: 1993-1995

Nevogilde House 1
Site: 2,150 sq. ft. (654 sq. mt.)
Building: 780 sq. ft. (237 sq. mt.)
Date of Design: 1982
Construction completed: 1985

Nevogilde House 2
Site: 9,850 sq. ft. (3000 sq. mt.)
Building: 1,150 sq. ft. (350 sq. mt.)
Date of Design: 1983
Construction completed: 1988

Alcanena House
Site: 164,000 sq. ft. (49,880 sq. mt.)
Building: 1,770 sq. ft. (540 sq. mt.)
Date of Design: 1987
Construction completed: 1992

Miramar House
Site: 11,800 sq. ft. (3,600 sq. mt.)
Building: 1,250 sq. ft. (380 sq. mt.)
Date of Design: 1987
Construction completed: 1991

Boavista Avenue House
Site: 1,750 sq. ft. (538 sq. mt.)
Building: 1,250 sq. ft. (380 sq. mt.)
Date of Design: 1987
Construction completed: 1994

Bom Jesus House
Site: 12,000 sq. ft. (3,670 sq. mt.)
Building: 1,380 sq. ft. (420 sq. mt.)
Date of Design: 1989
Construction completed: 1994

Baião House
Site: 69,000 sq. ft. (21,000 sq. mt.)
Building: 395 sq. ft. (120 sq. mt.)
Date of Design: 1990-1991
Construction completed: 1991-1993

Maia House
Site: 2,400 sq. ft. (724 sq. mt.)
Building: 970 sq. ft. (296 sq. mt.)
Date of Design: 1990-1991
Construction completed: 1991-1993

Tavira House
Site: 18,700 sq. ft. (5,700 sq. mt.)
Building: 515 sq. ft. (157 sq. mt.)
Date of Design: 1991
Construction completed: 1994

Mies House Pavilions and Addition Pavilion
Project Staff: Kent Larson
Site: 5.5 acres (2 hectares)
Building: 2,050 sq. ft. (184.5 sq. mt.)
Date of Design: 1981
Construction completed: 1986
Addition
Project Staff: Kent Larson
Partner: Cary Davis
Building: 1,500 sq. ft. (184.5 sq. mt.)
Date of Design: 1985
Construction completed: 1989

Farmhouse with Lap Pool and Sunken Garden
Project Staff: Fritz Read, Jim Walker
Site: 500 acres (200 hectares)
Building: 5,000 sq. ft. (450 sq. mt.)
Date of Design: 1992
Construction completed: 1995

Bohan Kemp Residence
Consultants: TT-CBM Engineers
General Contractor: Mead Construction
Site: 0.5 acre (0.2 hectares)
Building: 1,900 sq. ft. (180 sq. mt.)
Date of Design: 1996
Construction completed: 1998

LaPoint Residence
Consultants: Stearn Joglekar Ltd.
General Contractor: Elder Jones Construction
Site: 0.5 acre (0.2 hectares)
Building: 3,100 sq. ft. (290 sq. mt.)
Date of Design: 1989-1990
Construction completed: 1990

Mussman Residence
Consultants: Stearn Joglekar Ltd.
General Contractor: Michigan City Associates
Site: 8,100 sq. ft. (750 sq. mt.)
Building: 3,750 sq. ft. (350 sq. mt.)
Date of Design: 1991
Construction completed: 1992

Essex Residence and Office
Consultants: LeMessurier Consultants, Inc.
General Contractor: Firehouse Construction
Site: 6,250 sq. ft. (580 sq. mt.)
Building: 4,400 sq. ft. (410 sq. mt.)
Date of Design: 1993
Construction completed: 1995

House on Deer Isle
Consultants: Zaldastani Associates, Inc.,
Goldman Associates, Inc.
General Contractor: Prin Allen and Sons
Site: 50 acres (20 hectares)
Building: 2,300 sq. ft. (214 sq. mt.)
Date of Design: 1984-1985
Construction completed: 1985

House on Great Cranberry Island
Consultants: Zaldastani Associates, Inc.
General Contractor: Victor Mercer, Inc.
Builder: Michael Westphal
Site: 4 acres (2 hectares)
Building: 3,000 sq. ft. (279 sq. mt)
Date of Design: 1985-1987
Construction completed: 1987

House on Potomac River
Consultants: Lewis H. Conklin
General Contractor: Peterson and Collins, Inc.
Builder: Michael Westphal
Site: 7,100 sq. ft. (660 sq. mt)
Building: 3,200 sq. ft. (297 sq. mt)
Date of Design: 1989-1992
Construction completed: 1992

Directory

House on Mount Desert Island
Consultants: Zaldastani Associates, Inc.,
Panitsas Associates, Inc.
General Contractor: John Ruger Associates
Site: 5 acres (2 hectares)
Building: 2,000 sq. ft. (186 sq. mt)
Date of Design: 1991-1993
Construction completed: 1993

House at Orcutt Harbor
Consultants: Zaldastani Associates, Inc.,
Panitsas Associates, Inc.
General Contractor: Phil Urban Fine Homes
Site: 5.1 acres (2 hectares)
Building: 3,700 sq. ft. (344 sq. mt)
Date of Design: 1991-1993
Construction completed: 1993

House in Surry
Consultants: Zaldastani Associates, Inc.,
Panitsas Associates, Inc.
General Contractor: Phil Urban Fine Homes
Site: 4 acres (1.6 hectares)
Building: 3,200 sq. ft. (297 sq. mt)
Date of Design: 1992-1993
Construction completed: 1995

Marquand Retreat
David Miller, Philip Christofides
Site: 200 acres (81 hectares)
Building: 450 sq. ft. (42 sq. mt.)
Construction completed: 1992

Campbell Residence
Craig Curtis, Amy Lelyveld
Site: 5 acres (2 hectares)
Building: 2,200 sq. ft. (204 sq. mt.)
Construction completed: 1994

Michaels/Sisson Residence
Robert Hull, Amy DeDominicis
Site: 2.5 acres (1 hectares)
Building: 2,400 sq. ft. (223 sq. mt.)
Construction completed: 1998

Opel Residence
Paul Aferiat, Reynolds Logan
Site: 12 acres (5 hectares)
Building: 2,700 sq. ft. (251 sq. mt)
Date of Design: 1985
Construction completed: 1987

Betchtler Residence
Bruce Donnally, Nancy Clayton,
Thomas Lewis, Sylvia Becker
Associate Architect: Pfister & Schiess Architekten
Site: 26,900 sq. ft. (2,500 sq. mt.)
Building: 10,225 sq. ft. (950 sq. mt.)
Date of Design: 1990
Construction completed: 1994

Alfredo DeVido Architects
412 East 85 Street
New York, NY 10028, USA
Tel: 212-517-6100
Fax: 212-517-6103
www.devido-architects.com
Email: adevido@devido-architects.com

Lacroze Miguens Prati
80 Shore Road
Cold Spring Harbor, NY 11724, USA
Tel: 631-692-4069
Fax: 631-692-9638
www.lmparchitects.com
Email: lacrozearch@netscape.net

Enrique Browne y Asociados, Arquitectos
Los Conquistadores 2461 Providencia
Santiago, Chile
Tel: 562-2342027
Fax: 562-2315630
Email: ebrowne@entelchile.net
www.arquitectura.com.ar/notas/browne/

Christian De Groote Arquitectos, Ltda.
Merced 22 Of. 801
Santiago Centro, Chile
Tel: 562-6330351
Fax: 562-6396608
Email: degrootem@ctcinternet.cl

Souto Moura –Arquitectos, Lda.
Rua do Aleixo, 53-1 A
4150-043 Porto Portugal
Tel: 351 22 6187547
Fax: 351 22 6108092
Email: souto.moura@mail.telepac.pt

Peter L. Gluck and Partners
646 West 131 Street
New York, NY 10027, USA
Tel: 212-690-4950
Fax: 212-690-4961
www.gluckpartners.com
Email: pgluck@gluckpartners.com

Peter Forbes, FAIA, Architects
12 Main Street
Seal Harbor, ME 04675, USA
Tel: 207-276-0970
Fax: 207-276-0971
Email: pfamaine@acadia.net

Viale Giovanni Milton 65
50129 Firenze, Italy
Tel: 39 055 46 27 457
Fax: 39 055 46 27 457
Email: pfafirenze@dada.it

Wheeler Kearns Architects
343 South Dearborn Suite 200
Chicago, IL 60604, USA
Tel: 312-939-7787
Fax: 312-939-5108
www.wkarch.com
Email: dan@wkarchl.com

The Miller/Hull Partnership
911 Western Avenue Room #220
Seattle, WA 98104, USA
Tel: 206-682-6837
Fax: 206-682-5692
www.millerhull.com
Email: ccurtis@millerhull.com

Gwathmey Siegel & Associates Architects, LLC
475 Tenth Avenue
New York, NY 10018, USA
Tel: 212-947-1240
Fax: 212-695-0886
www.gwathmey-siegel.com
Email: s.innone@gwathmey-siegel.com

Photographic Credits

Luis Ferreira Alves/Eduardo Souto Moura-Arquitectos, Lda., 142-154; 156-165; 166-173; 174-181; 182-191; 192-197; 198-205; 206-211

Alfonso Barrios/Enrique Browne y Asociados, Arquitectos, 54-63

©Richard Bryant, Arcaid/Gwathmey Siegel & Associates Architects, LLC, 330-339; 340-349

Steve Cridland/The Miller/Hull Partnership, 308; 312

Christian DeGroote Arquitectos, Ltda., 65-67; 80; 83 (top); 137 (center)

Camila del Fiero/Christian DeGroote Arquitectos, Ltda., 98 (bottom right) 99-107; 118 (bottom); 132

Ernie Duncan/The Miller/Hull Partnership, 318

Paul Ferrino/Peter Forbes, FAIA, Architects, 260-263; 267-268; 288; 290; 292-293

Scott Frances, ESTO/ Peter Forbes, FAIA, Architects, 280-285

Art Grice/The Miller/Hull Partnership, 326 (top); 327-329

Fred Housel/The Miller/Hull Partnership, 310; 316-317; 319 (bottom) 320-323; 324-326 (bottom)

Tim Hursley, The Arkansas Office/Peter Forbes, FAIA, Architects, 264-265; 269; 270-279

Mark Joseph/Wheeler Kearns Architects, 252; 258 (bottom)

William Kildow/Wheeler Kearns Architects, 230-235; 236-243; 244; 247; 250-251; 253; 255-258 (top); 259

George Lambros/Wheeler Kearns Architects, 248

Juan Manaut/Christian DeGroote Arquitectos, Ltda., 91

Norman McGrath/Alfredo DeVido Architects, 8-17

Norman McGrath/Peter L. Gluck and Partners, 212; 214-221

The Miller/Hull Partnership, 309; 311; 313-315

Eduardo Souto Moura-Arquitectos, Lda., 155

Gustavo Sosa Pinilla/Lacroze Miguens Prati, 18-25; 26-35; 36-43

Luis Poirot/Enrique Browne y Asociados, Arquitectos, 44-53

Luis Poirot/Christian DeGroote Arquitectos, Ltda., Fajnzylber House, 2, 78-79; 81-82; 83 (bottom); 85; 92; 94-97; 114-115; 117; 126-128 (top); 129 (top); 130-131; 133

James Steinkamp © Steinkamp/Ballogg Chicago/Wheeler Kearns Architects, (model shots), 246-247

Paul Warchol/Peter Forbes, FAIA, Architects, 286-287; 289; 291

Paul Warchol/Peter L. Gluck and Partners, 213; 222-229

Guy Wenborne/Christian DeGroote Arquitectos, Ltda., 64; 68-69; 70-77; 84; 86-90; 93; 108-113; 116; 118-121; 122-125; 134-137 (bottom); 138-141

Nick Wheeler/Peter Forbes, FAIA, Architects, 294-301; 302-307

Wheeler Kearns Architects, 245; 249; 254